MY FRIEND, JULIA LATHROP

M. Hamilton.

JANE ADDAMS

My Friend, Julia Lathrop

INTRODUCTION BY
ANNE FIROR SCOTT

University of Illinois Press

URBANA AND CHICAGO

FRONTISPIECE
Julia Lathrop, by A. Hamilton

First Illinois edition, 2004
© 1935, renewed 1963 by the Estate of Jane Addams
Reprinted by permission of John A. Brittain
Introduction © 2004 by Anne Firor Scott
Manufactured in the United States of America
1 2 3 4 5 C P 5 4 3 2 1

∞ This book is printed on acid-free paper.

Library of Congress Cataloging-in-Publication Data
Addams, Jane, 1860–1935.
My friend, Julia Lathrop / Jane Addams ; introduction by Anne Firor
Scott.— 1st Illinois ed.
        p.   cm.
Originally published: New York : Macmillan, 1935.
Includes index.
ISBN 0-252-02900-3 (cloth : alk. paper)
ISBN 0-252-07168-9 (pbk. : alk. paper)
1. Lathrop, Julia Clifford, 1858–1932. 2. Women in charitable work—
United States—Biography. 3. Women social reformers—United
States—Biography. I. Title.
HV28.L35A5   2004
362.7′92—dc21   2003010931

Contents

Introduction

ANNE FIROR SCOTT

✒ It is doubtful that many people strolling through a book store or reading publishers' advertisements will recognize the name Julia Lathrop. Yet she was one of the people who shaped the social and political history of the United States in the era historians label "progressive." Born in 1858, she came to adulthood at a time when a number of women were emerging into public leadership, working collectively and achieving considerable political and social power. Among these she was a towering figure.

It was a time of rapid change as cities grew, factories multiplied, immigrants flooded in, and communication and transportation speeded up. These changes brought new wealth, but they also brought complex social, economic, and political problems. The emergence of women as initiators of much social reform was the result of a long social process. During the 1830s women had begun to join temperance societies; during the 1840s a handful of the most daring set forth a declaration, detailing the constraints of law and custom that hampered them and calling for better education, more respect, and the right to vote. Perhaps most important of all, women invented the all-female voluntary association as a tool for circumventing these constraints. After the Civil War, doors to higher education began to open as colleges for women were established and coeducation became more common at existing institutions. By the 1890s, the first generation of women college graduates was reaching maturity. In colleges and universities they had developed a broader of view of what a woman might do in the world. Many were not content to live with their parents and wait for a suitable husband to appear.

Julia Lathrop was almost the epitome of the kind of woman shaped by this historical sequence. She had grown up in a family of reformers, with an antislavery father and a seminary-graduate mother. Both parents had supported her wish to go to Vassar, the first of the new women's colleges, and later her father welcomed her into his law office as what we would now call a paralegal. Raised to believe in social responsibility, she was attracted to a new experiment beginning in Chicago—the settlement known as Hull-House opened in 1889 by Jane Addams and Ellen Gates Starr to provide a place where educated middle-class women could live in an immigrant neighborhood and work toward building a bridge between members of their own class and working people, many of whom lived in Chicago's Nineteenth Ward. In the 1880s and 1890s Chicago may have been the most vibrant, as well as the most complex, urban setting in the United States. Certainly it was a place where unplanned, dynamic capitalism showed its worst as well as its best side. Its social problems could easily match those of Dickens's London, while its Gold Coast, so-called, housed the opulent families who had benefited dramatically from the city's energetic growth.

Over the years, numbers of women and men would be attracted to Hull-House. Two of these, Florence Kelley and Alice Hamilton, would join Addams and Lathrop to form a long-lasting inner circle. Lillian Wald, head of the Nurses' Settlement in New York, became their close associate.

From the early 1890s until their deaths these five were a formidable group of activists, leaders in what Robyn Muncy has labeled the "female dominion in American reform."[1] They had ideas about what the country needed and worked hard and effectively to put them into concrete programs. Although in time members of the Hull-House inner circle worked elsewhere—Kelley in New York, Lathrop in Washington, and Hamilton in Boston—Hull-House remained their anchor. Wald carried on her work on Henry Street until her death. Unusually talented individually (each in a different way), together they constituted a remarkable force.

Four left memoirs and have been the subjects of scholarly biographies. Julia Lathrop, the one each of the others described as her closest friend and whose multiple achievements could fill a very long book, left no memoir and has yet to attract a scholarly biographer. It is therefore particularly fortunate that this book, written so soon after Lathrop's death and just before Addams's own, should now be restored to print. It is important for layperson and historian alike.

My Friend is engagingly written and deceptively simple. The author's skill in choosing anecdotes, some of which only she could have known, for example, the incident of securing bread for immigrants en route to the United States (pp. 104–5), and her effective use of Lathrop's own words evoke her friend's way of looking at life. Addams and Lathrop— so alike in background yet so different in personality—shared a warm friendship and great mutual respect. Each credited the other for many of her own accomplishments. Addams remarked that writing this book was like rewriting her own autobiography from a different angle, and it does indeed throw a great deal of light on her thinking as well as on the extraordinary group of which she was the central figure. By the end a reader has gained some sense of the members of the Hull-House group and of Wald, who moves in and out of the narrative. The book also tells a good deal about the way the five women reinforced each other.

The opening chapter suggests Addams's assumptions about the forces that shape a personality. In search of foreshadowing genes, she writes at length about Lathrop's forebears. Some ancestors had been reform-minded, as were her parents. Lathrop's father had been an early member of the Republican Party when it was committed to antislavery, and both of her parents supported woman suffrage. Later chapters deal with all the major phases of Julia Lathrop's life except for the period when she was chief of the U.S. Children's Bureau. Grace Abbott, Lathrop's protégé who succeeded her in the post, had agreed to write a separate book about those nine years but never did so. The story has been only partly filled in by recent scholarship.[2]

It was no part of Addams's purpose to paint a picture, as the saying goes, "warts and all." When a modern scholarly biography is someday written, we will learn that Julia Lathrop, despite her extraordinary spirit and basic optimism about human behavior, had periods of despair when she felt herself to be a failure. Her private letters reveal that she was under no illusions about human nature. Her famous wit, which was never used destructively on vulnerable people, could be biting indeed when she spoke of or to corrupt or insensitive people in positions of power.[3] But of all that Addams says little.

Nor does Addams, as a modern historian might, probe for unconscious sources of motivation. How, for example, did Lathrop, raised in
middle-class comfort, come to be so empathetic with immigrants and
others in dire poverty? And how did she, a single career woman, become
so deeply committed to child welfare? With the perspective of time and
as collections of manuscripts not known to her contemporaries have become available, scholars have tried to understand the politics and methods of these reform-minded women. A complex analysis of Lathrop and
her world is beginning to take shape.[4] This book, written out of love and
sorrow, reveals how that world appeared to its inhabitants.

From her own experience Addams understood what it was like to
grow up in a small Illinois town. When Lathrop's father allowed her
to work in his law office, he recognized, as not all fathers of the time
did, that an educated woman might aspire to fields hitherto considered exclusively male. It was perhaps a reflection of her Vassar education that Lathrop's first undertaking at Hull-House was a Plato Club,
designed for the Greeks among their neighbors.

Philosophy, literature, music, and debating societies would continue
to be part of the Hull-House program, but before long the young wom-
en were introduced to a world of complex social problems far beyond
what they had understood at the outset. Chicago, growing at breakneck
speed, had a full array: robber barons, political struggles, urban "bood-
lers," ward bosses, children without schools, children who worked in
dangerous places, uncertain employment, white-slavery scares, filthy
streets, mounds of garbage, swelling numbers of immigrants from
many parts of the world who struggled to find a place in a new country, and huge gaps between rich and poor.

The great depression that followed so closely upon the famous Columbian Exposition of 1893 was a powerful learning experience for Hull-
House residents. While they all searched for ways to help their neighbors in that time of dire need, Lathrop decided to volunteer as a "county
visitor" and set out to educate herself about the institutions Cook
County had created to care for people unable to take care of themselves.
Just four years after her arrival in Chicago she described the experience
in graphic detail in a pioneering social study, *Hull House Maps and Papers*.[5] She provided descriptions and statistics and at the same time

painted a picture of life in the poorhouse (euphemistically called the "infirmary") that might touch even the most cynical politician:

> The absolute lack of privacy, the monotony and dulness, [sic] the discipline, the enforced cleanliness,—these are the inevitable and, in the opinion of some, the wholesome disadvantages of the infirmary from the standpoint of the inmate. There is not a common sitting room for men or for women in the whole great place; the supply of books and papers is so small as scarcely to be visible. Occasionally one may see a group of men playing cards upon a bed in one corner of a ward and the old fellows have a tobacco allowance; but any provision for homely comfort, for amusements or distractions from themselves and their compulsory neighbors is wanting, alike for the most decent and the most worthless. . . . If husbands and wives are obliged to go to the infirmary they are always separated, no matter how aged and infirm, nor how blameless.[6]

In 1893, appointed by Gov. John Peter Altgeld as the first woman on the State Board of Charities, Lathrop moved on to make a similarly careful study of each of the 102 state institutions for the old, disabled, mentally ill, or orphaned and undertook the uphill work of trying to make them function better. She served on the board until 1909, with only one four-year hiatus. Alice Hamilton's anecdote about their joint visit to one institution provides a memorable example of Lathrop's relationships with the people in charge (p. 61).

By long tradition, politicians considered jobs in such institutions as opportunities for the party in power to reward the politically faithful. Very early Lathrop recognized that the custom led to the appointment of totally or partly unqualified people and was a major cause of the failings she so graphically described. Thus was born her lifelong commitment to the merit system. Her views made many enemies among politicians who had built their careers on the practice of rewarding supporters. Convincing successive governors and, later, political leaders in Washington of the virtues of merit over patronage became an ongoing effort.[7]

As her experience and her reach extended, Lathrop became a moving spirit in Illinois for improving care for those who were least able to care for themselves. Influenced by the growing movement for a systematic "social science" she not only undertook careful examination of conditions in the institutions for which the board was responsible but also tried to learn about possible ways to solve the problems she identified.[8] At her own expense, she traveled to Scotland and France to search for methods that might be useful in her home state.

From Toqueville's time, astute observers recognized the American tendency to form voluntary associations. As the nineteenth century came to a close, the creation of formal institutions to deal with social problems began to join voluntary associations as a characteristic American endeavor.

Julia Lathrop and her colleagues contributed to that trend. When she saw a need, her instinct was to join with other like-minded people to create an institution to address that need. During her first twenty years at Hull-House, she played a leading role in creating, among other organizations, the Juvenile Court, the Juvenile Protective Association, the Immigrants Protective League, the Chicago School of Civics and Philanthropy, and the National Committee for Mental Hygiene. Each institutional achievement was a story in itself. Addams describes the beginnings in 1899 of what has been called the world's first juvenile court. In so doing, she highlights many of Lathrop's defining characteristics: persistence, the ability to learn from and work with others, and knowing the people who would be helpful in any given enterprise.

In this case, Lathrop's co-worker was Lucy Flower, an older social worker who had become a friend and mentor. Sharing the conviction that the prevailing methods of dealing with juvenile offenders were destructive, the two went to work to create a new kind of court that would be concerned not with punishment but with identifying sources of misbehavior and finding ways to deal with them. Women across the state were mobilized to press for the necessary legislation. The Illinois legislature passed the bill but neglected to appropriate money to carry out its provisions. Nothing daunted, the founders turned again to other women, especially members of the Chicago Woman's Club and other voluntary associations, this time asking them to provide the infrastructure required if the court were to function. Members of a volunteer Juvenile Court Committee raised money to pay a judge and a probation officer and provide a place for the children to live while awaiting their turns in court.

In time, after the court had begun to prove its value, the county took over its funding, and the Juvenile Court Committee transformed itself into the Juvenile Protective Association, an organization dedicated to providing help for the most vulnerable children in the poorest districts of the city. The association continued to function for many years, providing much valuable data for the developing child welfare movement and later for the federal Children's Bureau.

When it turned out that although many children responded well to the new institution some inevitably did not, Lathrop turned to Ethel Sturges Dummer, an independent philanthropist who had great interest in mental health. Together they created a Psychopathic Institution for Children, described here by its first director as "blazing a new trail" in child welfare (p. 99).[9]

The next institution-building project was again vintage Lathrop. Dedicated to the idea that administrators of welfare institutions should be trained for the job, she worked with Graham Taylor, a faculty member of the Chicago Theological School and head of the well-known settlement called the Chicago Commons. Taylor had been a pioneer in the training of social workers for several years before founding what would become the Chicago School of Civics and Philanthropy. He drew Lathrop, whom he greatly admired, into the enterprise to establish a research department. The school was launched in 1907, and she immediately set out to persuade the new Russell Sage Foundation that it should help pay for her department.[10] When the money came, she recruited and trained an unusually talented young woman, Sophinisba Breckinridge, who had degrees in law, political science, and economics, to take over her job. Together they persuaded Edith Abbott, another University of Chicago Ph.D. in economics then teaching at Wellesley College, to join the faculty.[11]

Breckinridge and Abbott were, like Lathrop, part of the rapidly growing movement for basing reform on systematic social science. With her blessing, they conducted and published a number of careful studies of social issues. One of these, for which Lathrop wrote the introduction, reported the results of a ten-year study of the families of children who had come through the Juvenile Court. The focus was less on children as problems than on the social and environmental situations in which children were likely to get in trouble with the law.[12]

Lathrop herself designed and taught a summer course for people who were or would be working in the various institutions she had come to know as a county visitor and member of the State Board of Charities. Then, she had argued vigorously about the need for trained people. Now, she would train a few. What she had observed in various welfare institutions also shaped her contributions to the school. She became a strong proponent of occupational therapy and was especially interested in the new field of mental hygiene. In 1909 she would be the only woman among the twelve charter members of the new National Committee for Mental Hygiene.[13]

Breckinridge and Abbott, mentored by Lathrop and Kelley, were part of the generation in which professionalism and research as the bases for action became basic values.[14] Their somewhat ruthless takeover of the School of Civics and Philanthropy (while Graham Taylor was away in California) in order to create a graduate school of social work at the University of Chicago provided a dramatic example of the changing nature of the discipline. Lathrop was ambivalent about this move on the part of her young protégés. Given her strong belief in the importance of systematic social science, she saw at once the advantage of a graduate program attached to a major university, one that would be, its founders hoped, on par with the university's schools of law and medicine. Yet she was also sensitive to Taylor's feelings. He had grown old in good works and had the highly personal approach to social work typical of the early settlement movement. Of course, he felt that he had been sandbagged by the younger generation. Lathrop not only understood his reaction but was also anxious to find a way that his contributions should not be denigrated or forgotten; she and Addams did what they could to that end.[15]

All along Lathrop was honing the characteristics that would shape her career: the ability to listen to all kinds of people, including those not like herself; skill in bringing together people of differing views to see what they might have in common; and a gift for politics in the best sense. She understood how to make things happen. Her characteristic methods, which Alice Hamilton had observed, would be repeated many times in various settings, including the office of the president of the United States. She had a gift for what we now call "networking." She knew the people whose hands were on the levers of power. Her ability to persuade was legendary, whether she was dealing with a long-time friend or a potential political adversary. Her letters to the Russell Sage Foundation seeking funds for a research department provide a good example of her gift for persuasion (pp. 107–9).

In such negotiations, as in so many others, Lathrop endeared herself to co-workers with what a long-time friend called "her divine sense of humor."[16] She was, Alice Hamilton would write, "The most companionable person, with a sense of the absurd and a way of telling absurd stories that was unique, and she had a large store of them gathered as she journeyed back and forth over Illinois during the many years she was on the State Board of Charities."[17] Enella Benedict, a long-time Hull-House resident, was the source of another revealing anecdote, a description of how Lathrop and Hamilton worked in tandem to promote Hamilton's own central interest—the dangers of toxic chemicals in the workplace (p. 62).

As firmly as Julia Lathrop believed in the possibilities of social science as the basis for dealing with social problems, she never thought research was an end in itself. The essence of her definition of the "scientific spirit" was science applied to human purposes. Once one had employed the prevailing scientific methods to discover the nature of a problem, the next step was to figure out how to solve it. In somewhat the same spirit, she never believed that passing a law was the end of a task. Only when there was adequate enforcement could she be satisfied. Late in life she would argue that what was called the "failure of prohibition" was in fact failure to enforce the Volstead Act, which had been intended to ensure that the provisions of the amendment be carried out.

Although she had none of the flamboyance of her close friend Florence Kelley, Lathrop had plenty of courage when the things in which she believed were at stake. Early in their collaboration, she and Kelley risked serious illness when they visited sickrooms during the smallpox epidemic that followed the Columbian Exposition. Although Lathrop had a reputation for caution, for trying to see every side of an issue, when she decided what was right she spoke her mind, although almost always diplomatically. A timid person could not have written the letter of resignation to Gov. Richard Yates printed on pages 78–80.

Throughout her life, Lathrop exhibited what Addams and Alice Hamilton both called "disinterested virtue." Of all the contemporaries who wrote about her, whether in private or in public, no one—even those who disagreed with her—ever identified the least self-interest in her work.[18] Despite her manifest intelligence and much-praised wit she was remarkably modest. Late in life she wrote to a woman who had asked for help in composing a talk. The letter begins, "I am a very much over-advertised person due to the fact that I chanced to be the first woman to be placed in charge of a government department."[19]

Of course there was no "chance" about it. The Children's Bureau had been created after years of lobbying led by Lillian Wald. The legend was that Wald and Florence Kelley, head of the National Consumers League and living at Henry Street, had come up with the idea over breakfast one morning when they saw an item in the newspaper about money being appropriated for the Department of Agriculture and intended to benefit farm animals. Why, the women asked, could not Congress do at least as much for children? The National Child Labor Committee, headed by men but including a number of women, joined the effort to support the proposed legislation. Women's organizations across the country were mobilized to lobby for the bill.

When Congress finally adopted legislation to create the Children's Bureau and the president signed it in April 1912, members of the Hull-House network went into action. They were convinced that Lathrop's skills were just what the unprecedented job required and wanted to make sure she would be appointed rather than one of several men who thought themselves just right for the position. Because the Republican Party was in power, it probably helped that Lathrop's family had been Republican since the party was created. The support of Julius Rosenwald, president of Sears Roebuck and a dedicated philanthropist who had worked closely with Lathrop and admired her work, also helped.[20] Ironically, Lathrop, the firm advocate for the merit system, gained office through the political skills of her friends.

No sooner was she in office, however, than she began to promote the idea that the new bureau was a scientific enterprise devoted to improving child welfare and that it should therefore be off limits for political appointments. Her success in making this point became evident when Woodrow Wilson won the White House shortly after her service began. Of course, "deserving Democrats" viewed jobs in a new bureau as their natural right. One senator was said to have inquired angrily of the new president, "Are we to understand, Mr. President, that it is your policy to retain Republicans and let good Democrats starve?" Wilson is said to have responded, "You may understand, Mr. Senator, that it is my policy to retain Miss Lathrop!"[21]

The woman who went to Washington appeared to be a proper middle-class lady. She was handsome and fond of good clothes but did not spend much time thinking about such things. She was not wealthy and lived frugally but was generous to those whose need touched her heart. She took her job seriously but did not take herself seriously. She was, above all, a tough, gifted politician. Shrewdly, using her knowledge of the Civil Service law in order to do what she had in mind, Lathrop appointed women to nearly every part of the infant bureau. "Women," she once remarked, "cannot afford to be incompetent." She also believed them better suited than men for work in welfare. She liked the idea of expanding the number of professional opportunities open to educated women. Although she never stated this as part of her purpose, her actions had that effect.[22]

By her second year in office, her political acumen was in evidence when Congress agreed to increase the bureau's appropriation sixfold and to nearly quadruple its staff. Lillian Wald, Jane Addams, and Florence Kelley, among others, helped mobilize women's organizations to support these increases, and members of Congress, whatever their private views of the Children's Bureau, were persuaded.[23]

Not only did the bureau have the distinction of being the first welfare institution created by the federal government, but under Lathrop's leadership it was also unique in the history of federal bureaus in the way it dealt with clients. William L. Chenery, who as a young man had lived at Hull-House and later became one of the nation's leading journalists, wrote at the end of Lathrop's term: "[The Children's Bureau was] an organization which, measured by farsighted purpose, instinctive loyalty to democracy, and capacity to achieve was almost without parallel in Washington . . . public officials who are wise leaders of the people and at the same time shining examples of effectual administration are all too few."[24]

Lathrop appointed women who shared her convictions, first that social reform should rest on careful collection of data and, second, that people in need were human beings rather than statistics. Understanding the potential of all-woman voluntary associations, Children's Bureau staff members from the first created close relationships with such associations across the country.[25]

Children's Bureau annual reports are filled with examples of the effectiveness of this strategy. Even with an enhanced budget, the bureau could not possibly have conducted comprehensive studies of infant mortality, child health, or the need for birth registration laws without the help of thousands—in at least one case, millions—of volunteers. By this means the bureau accomplished much work at a small cost in dollars and created an unprecedented relationship between women and the federal government. Moreover, it developed a vast and reliable lobby to support additional appropriations and child welfare legislation.[26]

With the help of volunteers, the women of the bureau established remarkable relationships with clients. Once they began distributing the first *Infant and Child Care* pamphlet, letters poured in from women across the country, asking for specific advice. Some years there were more than a hundred thousand letters—and each was answered with advice.[27] In some cases, Lathrop or a member of the staff recruited a volunteer in the letter-writer's community who would seek her out and offer such help as could be given.[28]

Although women on the staff tried hard to be helpful and often showed great empathy for the letter-writers, their proffered advice was not always precisely appropriate to clients' needs. It was sometimes difficult for career women, mostly middle class, mostly college-educated, and mostly single, to fully understand the lives of working-class or farm wives who had too many children, too little money, and unsympathetic husbands. Advising such women to give their children safe milk and fresh vegetables, to rest in the afternoons, and to make sure the children took naps hardly constituted practical information. The prevailing assumptions of at least some of the professional women are suggested by a notation in the [*First*] *Annual Report:* "The aim of the bureau has been in every case to place at the service of the correspondents the best information now available on the subject . . . or references to the best sources. . . . The demands of the correspondence have necessitated compiling . . . provisional lists of institutions to meet special request and brief lists of authorities on special subjects."[29] It is hard to imagine that many clients had access to "references to the best sources" or to the authorities on the brief lists.

Still, the desperation of need made hope hard to dampen. The letters, which poured in, repeated stories of more children than a woman could cope with and are similar to those Margaret Sanger collected for *Motherhood in Bondage*. Indeed, many writers begged for contraceptive advice. Unlike Sanger, however, Children's Bureau women were not willing to break the law by giving it. Congress would have abandoned the bureau in a moment had it officially recommended limiting pregnancy or described the use of contraceptives. Replies to questions about the morality of abortion left no doubt that staff members opposed that practice.

Reflecting on what was sometimes a missed connection between middle-class women and their working-class and rural constituents raises a complex set of issues about the way some progressive reformers viewed the world and what constituted their basic attitudes toward poor people. Although Lathrop and her colleagues shared profound concern for those at the bottom of the heap and spent their lives trying to improve such lives, it is nonetheless possible to read a faint undertone of noblesse oblige into some of their words, especially those written when the women were just beginning their careers.

That was rarely true of Addams, who all her adult life wanted to help people to help themselves. She worked closely with a number of working-class women who felt that she treated them as equals. Lathrop's early views were perhaps more class-conscious. Writing in 1895, she spoke of the inmates of county institutions as "human wastage" and described the ward in which Hull-House existed as containing "the least adaptable of foreign populations . . . living in every sort of maladjustments."[30] Her descriptions included a number of what we now call ethnic stereotypes. Very soon, however, she began to recognize more clearly the interaction of circumstances and personal inadequacy.

As she worked and learned, Lathrop's views became more complex, and she moved away from focusing on whether the poor were responsible for their own conditions to examining the outside forces that shaped their lives. By the 1920s she was convinced that the basic social problem was poverty and that public policy at all levels of government could and should undertake to eliminate it. "I am sure," she wrote to Lillian Wald, "that every person who thinks must feel driven to the conviction that poverty is the baffling but relentless enemy of children and that our minds must be turned toward the methods of discovering and setting up a just—economically just—social order if we are to have more than a spasmodic and superficial progress for the young."[31]

It is difficult to separate conscious from unconscious assumptions among the women in Lathrop's circle. The merit system clearly benefited people like themselves, educated, capable administrators, at the expense of "corrupt" bosses who arguably had a better understanding of the needs of poor people. Jane Addams understood and analyzed that issue very early in the history of Hull-House, and echoes of her analysis appear in some of Lathrop's writing.[32]

If the bureau's staff, and, by implication, Lathrop herself, sometimes missed the mark with clients, they had excellent insight into the minds and habits of politicians. From the earliest days, certain members of Congress vehemently attacked the idea of a bureau for children. The early increase in its appropriation was a tribute not to the sudden conversion of many legislators but to the political effectiveness of as-yet mostly voteless women across the country, whom bureau supporters had mobilized. For the first fifteen years or so of its existence, the bureau's troops were more effective than those of the opposition, and they moved briskly to fulfill their agenda. Lathrop was not universally loved, of course. Employers of child labor and exploited women workers, rabid anti-suffragists, medical doctors jealous of their prerogatives, and politicians who opposed the merit system were among her severest critics. They did not constitute, on the whole, a group with whom history has dealt kindly.

Lathrop's response to the challenge of U.S. entry into what was then called the Great War was typical of her skill in turning the unexpected to advantage. She immediately began to say that nothing was more necessary to the country at war, especially in view of the poor health of so many young men summoned by draft boards, than a program to improve children's health. She persuaded President Wilson to make a statement to the effect that patriotism, next to support for the soldiers, demanded work for child welfare. The president added $229,000 from his war emergency fund to the resources for this purpose.

War brought millions of women out to roll bandages, save food, and knit sweaters for the troops. Lathrop drew on this pool of women who wanted to do something useful, and in 1918 the Children's Bureau inaugurated a Year of the Child.[33] Once again, volunteers were summoned, this time to weigh and measure children all over the country. The bureau helped develop standards for height and weight and arranged physical examinations for thousands of children whose ailments were identified and treated. Eleven million women were said to have been involved. Many state and local agencies also helped. A revolution in the prevailing assumptions about public responsibility for child welfare was carried out without much fanfare.[34] The bureau also seized the opportunity to push for a major element in its child welfare program. As they examined the issue of children's health, both the volunteers and the bureau staff dwelt especially on the need to get children out of the workplace and into school.

Long before the creation of the Children's Bureau, its founders had been convinced that limits should be set on the use of children in industry. Florence Kelley had written of her youthful exposure to the work of young boys in the glass industry, and the work of children in southern textile mills had long been a concern of southern reformers. Because industries in many states depended on cheap child labor, it was a touchy political issue.

In 1916, and with strong support from the Children's Bureau and many of its female supporters, Congress had passed, and President Wilson signed, the Keating-Owens bill, which prohibited the products of child labor from entering interstate and foreign commerce. The bureau set out immediately to implement the law, and Lathrop persuaded Grace Abbott, younger sister of Edith and a long-time collaborator in matters dealing with immigrants, to come to Washington and take charge of the program. Enforcement was hardly underway when the Supreme Court, in *Hammer v. Dagenhart,* declared the child labor law unconstitutional on the grounds that it improperly rested on the right of Congress to regulate interstate commerce and as such represented a dangerous invasion of state's rights.

The next challenge to supporters of the cause was to devise a bill that would pass muster. Sympathetic lawyers consulted each other and agreed that their best hope was to devise a bill based on congressional power to lay and collect taxes. Julia Lathrop had grave doubts about that approach. She was sure that the Treasury Department, if assigned to enforce child labor restrictions, would not do so energetically. There seemed no readily available alternative, however, and Congress was persuaded to pass such a bill. By 1922 the issue became moot when the new law was also declared unconstitutional. The Court, quite rightly, said that it was not primarily a tax law but a means of changing national policy and as such was unacceptable. Only one road was left: Supporters faced the daunting task of devising and pushing through a constitutional amendment and then working for its ratification.

Even among reformers who share a goal, turf wars can limit effectiveness. The women ranged behind Lathrop, Florence Kelley, and Lillian Wald did not have great respect for the National Child Labor Committee and maneuvered to keep the campaign in their own hands. The NCLC returned the compliment. In the end, and despite this tug-of-war, Congress did pass the amendment. Although there was a determined effort by newly enfranchised women, led by the Women's Joint Congressional Committee and especially by the National League of Women Voters, ratification was never achieved. Their work was not entirely wasted, however. When the New Deal came along, child labor was at last restricted.[35]

In the meantime, Lathrop was more successful when she undertook to choose her successor and persuade the secretary of labor and Congress to go with her choice. The job was an attractive one to Republicans returning to power after eight years. The Children's Bureau, Lathrop wrote, was "considered the jewel of the Department of Labor" and hence "good trading stock." Long, handwritten letters to her sister on the subject provide a fascinating case study in political acumen. She reported "many confidential talks" with various powerful politicians in both houses of Congress. She also advised her chosen candidate, Grace Abbott, to write to as many "rockribbed Republican friends" as she could find. When the secretary of labor told her that "many wonderful letters" in support of other women had reached his desk, she informed Abbott, "It is time to put on our armor and set to." Lathrop enlisted her good friend Harriet Taylor Upton, an old suffrage co-worker whom she much admired—calling her "the best person in Washington for honesty and fairness and humor"—and now head of the women's division of the Republican Party. Women from both parties were called to action, and the well-oiled Hull-House machine did its part. In due course, Grace Abbott was appointed and confirmed.[36]

So it was that in 1921 Lathrop moved back to Illinois, ready to become reacquainted with all that was going on there and prepared to
help organize the newly enfranchised women for their responsibilities
as citizens. She spoke to enthusiastic groups of women all over the state,
advising them to take nothing for granted, work hard, and vote intelligently. She agreed to be president of the Illinois League of Women
Voters and was soon at work in the legislature. She was also for a time
vice president of the National League of Women Voters. The league's
early program was made to order for her because it included support
for the merit system and for a child labor amendment to the Constitution. At both levels of league activity, Lathrop was a strong voice for
its defining principle: study first, then act on sound knowledge (p. 146).

Of Lathrop's role, the historian of the League of Women Voters
would write: "Jane Addams' influence in shaping the ideas and releas-
ing the moral energies of the leaders in the last phases of the suffrage
movement can hardly be overstated. From the brilliant circle of women
in her orbit, the League of Women Voters drew not only a large part
of its program but a majority of its early officers . . . the greatest of
these early vice presidents, Julia Lathrop, was her closest associate."[37]

Although she had turned the Children's Bureau over to her successor, Lathrop continued to watch over the agency. She and Abbott were
in constant communication about every issue within the bureau as well
as the legislative program of the recently enfranchised women. She participated in the strategic defense of the bureau, which, as it had long
been, was attacked and subjected to a good many efforts to clip its
wings. Lathrop and Abbott exchanged long letters, addressing each
other in Hull-House fashion as "Dear GA" "Dear J. Lathrop." Despite
their differences in style, the two appear to have been entirely compat-
ible. There is no hint in the correspondence that Abbott resented so
much attention from her predecessor and mentor. She had learned the
political game well and carried on the tradition of political effectiveness during the early part of the difficult 1920s. Comparing the two, Lela
Costin later observed, "Julia Lathrop used persuasion and even cajol-
ery and made her points in a circuitous way with frequent expressions
of empathy for another's point of view. Grace Abbott was forthright,
sometimes abrupt, immediately direct . . . [yet] each possessed administrative ability . . . each had a sense of humor in daily affairs."[38]

Even before she left the bureau, Lathrop had been deeply involved in planning for the first major legislative project of the now-enfranchised women, one that again depended heavily on the well-organized network of voluntary associations. The Sheppard-Towner bill, which aimed to create a federal-state program for improving the health of mothers and children, embodied what the Children's Bureau had learned in the first decade of its existence about mothers and children's pressing needs for health care. It also encompassed the thinking of the Hull-House circle about child welfare and federal-state cooperation.

As early as 1917 Lathrop had developed a plan, which in most essentials was included in the legislation. Introduced by Sen. Morris Sheppard, a progressive Democrat from Texas, and Rep. Horace Towner, a Republican from Iowa, the bill immediately aroused the ire of some medical men who thought no women's organization could possibly provide what was, they asserted, their special responsibility. The fact that so many women and children were without access to necessary care suggested that the responsibility had not been very effectively met.

Activists among the new women voters were filled with zeal, and members of Congress were yet in doubt as to just how much they had to fear from these new citizens. Visible leadership for the bill came from the Women's Joint Congressional Committee, which brought together representatives from a wide range of women's organizations, from the most radical to very conservative. Within the group the League of Women Voters, the General Federation of Women's Clubs, the Women's Christian Temperance Union, and the National Consumers League were most active in developing grass-roots support for the Sheppard-Towner bill, which as a result passed by overwhelming majorities in both houses. Lathrop believed that the data about the health needs of mothers and children that the bureau had gathered during its first decade of existence had laid the groundwork for this success.[39]

As the 1920s wore on, attacks on the Children's Bureau became ever more virulent. Somehow it had become a target during the so-called Red Scare that followed the Russian revolution. A paranoid group calling itself Women Patriots told the world that the bureau housed subversive social workers trained at Hull-House and taking orders from the Soviet Union.[40] In its view, the Sheppard-Towner Act represented a communist plot. No reform group was immune from attack. Even the

Women's Christian Temperance Union and the League of Women Voters were included in the notorious "spider web chart" that purported to prove the communist ties of nearly every women's organization other than the Women Patriots.

Efforts to transfer vital functions of the bureau to other branches of the government continued with strong support from some members of the medical establishment. Small-town and rural doctors who were in direct contact with poor women, many of whom had participated in the Year of the Child, were likely to support the bureau; urban specialists and organizations such as the American Medical Association were another matter.

As late as 1929, as opposition from the medical establishment grew, Lathrop urged Jane Addams "as one of the creators of the Children's Bureau" to defend the notion that child welfare was a great deal more than health. She enlisted Belle Sherwin, president of the League of Women Voters, to help defend the bureau as the appropriate center of federal child welfare activities. Another league leader, Mrs. Louis Slade, who had good relations with President Herbert Hoover, arranged for him to see Lathrop to discuss the future of the bureau. Hoover was not sympathetic. The glory days of the bureau were over until its work, so well done, reemerged as a shaping force in the New Deal.

Meanwhile, somewhat reluctantly, Lathrop had agreed to represent the United States on the Child Welfare Committee of the League of Nations. It was a difficult assignment because the United States was not a league member, and the role of its representative was ambiguous. In letters to Abbott she expressed considerable frustration and doubts about accomplishing anything. In retrospect, however, the record shows that she had considerable influence on the league and played an important part in spreading the gospel of child welfare to women in many parts of the world.

As if child labor and the League of Nations were not enough, Lathrop was also involved with a Committee to Study Ports of Entry—that is, with the question of how immigrants were received when they arrived. Next to the welfare of children, it was a topic close to her heart.

Although her activity seemed unabated, by the late 1920s family correspondence increasingly revealed concern for Julia Lathrop's health. The concern was justified. Something was wrong, and not long after the death of her dear friend Florence Kelley she found herself in need of a goiter operation. Her reply to a letter of concern from Katherine Lenroot conveys much of her spirit: "[The news was] better than I feared and . . . there is strategic value in having no great immunity from the common lot."[41] She died the next day.

To their reform ideology Julia Lathrop and her friends managed to add a set of operational procedures and used them to great effect. They also managed to pass them along to the next generation of women who came under their influence. For a few years, from about 1910 until the economic breakdown of 1929, this group of American women exercised hitherto unprecedented political leverage. Further, some of those they trained made vital contributions to the agenda of Franklin Roosevelt's New Deal.

If we could ask them, How did you do it? they might have said simply that the times were right and that their achievements rested upon the work of millions of women. The mysteries of leadership are not altogether understood, nor are what we call "social forces." A few things, however, are clear from the record. The women believed in the power of knowledge. Lathrop herself laid great stress on what she conceived to be social-scientific data, although even more significant was her knowledge of human nature. Women trained at Hull-House made it their practice to know more about the subject at hand then the people they hoped to convince. Knowledge was important for analysis of problems and also a significant tool for political effectiveness. They also came to understand that the welfare of children or women depended a great deal on building social structures that minimized poverty. They viewed government as an agency for helping people. Finally, they developed techniques for public-private cooperation, not between government and corporations but between government and citizen volunteers.

A much longer discussion than this one would be required to trace the evolution of public policies dealing with child welfare from the 1930s to the present. Systems and programs for the benefit of children abound, but problems have also grown apace. The combined state and federal spending for children's health now runs into billions annually. Yet Lathrop's conviction that programs for children's welfare could not have lasting effects until the nation solves the problem of poverty is as true now as it was then. Marian Wright Edelman, inventor and leader of the Children's Defense Fund, is in some sense a spiritual descendant of Julia Lathrop. In 2002 she wrote, "The U.S. leads the world in the number of millionaires and billionaires and in gross domestic product. Yet its children are the poorest group—a moral tumor on America's soul . . . some counties in the United States have an astounding 3 out of 5 children living in poverty."[42]

The basic principles on which Lathrop and her circle operated are still relevant in our vastly more complex world. This book is a powerful reminder of their work.

NOTES

1. Robyn Muncy, *Creating a Female Dominion in American Reform, 1890–1935* (New York: Oxford University Press, 1991).

2. Dorothy Bradbury's *Five Decades of Action for Children: A History of the Children's Bureau* (Washington: Department of Health, Education and Welfare, 1962), which is brief and factual, includes some illuminating quotations from Julia Lathrop.

3. The primary sources for a biography of Lathrop are extensive. They include many of her long, handwritten letters now in the Abbott Papers in the Regenstein Library at the University of Chicago and in the Rockford College Archives in Rockford, Illinois. Her official correspondence from the Children's Bureau days is in the National Archives. Her annual reports as chief are illuminating, as are the reflections of many of the people with whom she worked.

4. Muncy's *Creating a Female Dominion* is an excellent study and has been of great help to me in trying to understand Julia Lathrop's career.

5. Julia Lathrop, *Hull House Maps and Papers* (New York: Thomas Y. Crowell, 1893). This study was carried out by the residents of Hull-House and was one of the earliest efforts to carefully study an immigrant community. Lathrop's essay is called "Cook County Charities." The project was the first of the urban studies for which sociologists in Chicago would become famous.

6. Lathrop, *Hull House Maps and Papers*, 149.

7. The subject of Civil Service reform had been agitated since the 1870s, but generally with respect to the federal bureaucracy. As Julia Lathrop grew, she must have been aware of arguments in favor of a merit system; her father was, according to Addams, dedicated to the idea of Civil Service reform.

8. Lathrop grew up at a time when modern social science was beginning to take shape. See Dorothy Ross, *The Origins of American Social Science* (New York: Cambridge University Press, 1991); and Mary O. Furner, *Advocacy and Objectivity: A*

Crisis in the Professionalization of American Social Science, 1895–1905 (Lexington: University Press of Kentucky, 1975).

9. For Dummer's biography, see *Notable American Women: The Modern Period*, ed. Barbara Sicherman and Carol Hurd Green (Cambridge: Harvard University Press, 1980), 208–10. A philanthropist, she had a strong interest in mental health. Her daughter, Katherine Dummer Fisher, became a leader in the Illinois League of Women Voters after suffrage.

10. Russell Sage, who had been one of the richest men in America, was not known for philanthropy. When he died, however, his wife established the foundation named for him, which was a pioneer in the collection of social statistics. It was a natural source of support for people who had Lathrop's convictions about the need for social science as the basis for social action.

11. A decade younger than Lathrop and Addams, these young women represented the further development of higher education for women. Both had advanced degrees from the University of Chicago; Breckinridge, indeed, had two. They were firm believers in the value of social science but, like Lathrop, considered it for the benefit of social reform. The following generation tended toward studying sociology as an academic discipline, split off from reform movements.

12. Lela B. Costin, *Two Sisters for Social Justice: A Biography of Grace and Edith Abbott* (Urbana: University of Illinois Press, 1983), 60–61.

13. The modern mental hygiene movement began with the publication of Clifford Whittingham Beers's *A Mind That Found Itself* (New York: Longmans Green, 1908) and his subsequent leadership in founding first the Connecticut Society for Mental Hygiene and then the National Committee for Mental Hygiene with the goals of improving attitudes toward mental illness, improving services for those who were mentally ill, and promoting studies that might lead to better mental health.

14. Robert Wiebe, *The Search for Order, 1877–1920* (New York: Hill and Wang, 1967), makes some thought-provoking speculations about this phenomenon. Wiebe does not, however, seem to understand the vital part women played in its creation.

15. Taylor had a remarkable career, although probably to Breckinridge and Abbott his ways seemed old-fashioned and insufficiently "scientific." For a measured and thorough study, see Louise C. Wade, *Graham Taylor: Pioneer for Social Justice, 1851–1938* (Chicago: University of Chicago Press, 1964).

16. At this point a reader might ask, Why not more examples of her famous wit? Unfortunately, humor is less likely to be recorded than, say, legislative achievements. Addams offers examples on pages 130, 143, and 146–47. Perhaps a careful search of Lathrop's voluminous correspondence would yield more examples, but on the whole we must take her friends' and admirers' word that she was indeed a person of remarkable wit.

17. Alice Hamilton, *Exploring the Dangerous Trades: The Autobiography of Alice Hamilton* (Boston: Little, Brown, 1943), 64.

18. Hamilton wrote, "When I try to describe Julia Lathrop the word that comes first to my mind is 'disinterested.' This is a rare quality, even in philanthropists, in people who are devoting their lives to others, for sacrifice and devotion can go with a certain kind of self-centeredness . . . Julia Lathrop did not see herself as the center of what she was doing" (*Exploring the Dangerous Trades*, 63).

19. Letter to "Dear Mrs. Johnson," Sept. 21, 1921, Julia Lathrop Papers, Rockford College, Rockford, Ill.

20. Julius Rosenwald was the genius behind the great success of Sears, Roebuck. He gave millions to help immigrants, African Americans, and others whom he perceived as needy. He had influence with the Republican Party and was a great admirer of Hull-House and its residents.

21. Quoted in Nancy P. Weiss, "Save the Children: A History of the Children's Bureau," Ph.D. diss., University of California at Los Angeles, 1973, 125.

22. Robyn Muncy believes this to have been a major purpose of Lathrop and her colleagues. That her decisions had that effect is beyond doubt; whether it was very much on her mind, however, is not altogether evident.

23. This story is dramatically recounted in Muncy, *Creating a Female Dominion*.

24. William L. Chenery, "A Great Public Servant," *Survey*, Sept. 1, 1921, 637–38.

25. This technique for circumventing society's restrictions forms a major theme of Anne Firor Scott, *Natural Allies: Women's Associations in American History* (Urbana: University of Illlinois Press, 1992).

26. The annual reports of the Children's Bureau are a mine of information about the way Lathrop and her staff proceeded. Among many other things, the reports include descriptions of how women's organizations were mobilized and the specific tasks they undertook.

27. See Molly Ladd-Taylor, *Raising a Baby the Government Way: Mothers' Letters to the Children's Bureau, 1915–1932* (New Brunswick: Rutgers University Press, 1986) for examples of the wide variety of letters to the bureau. Writers ranged from being virtually illiterate to being highly educated and from living in urban centers to residing in rural areas and on the frontier.

28. "Early in 1915, a little girl . . . wrote 'Uncle Sam' asking him to please 'send a baby brother whenever you have any in!' . . . [Julia Lathrop] wrote: 'I wish I had a baby brother to send too such a good home as I am sure he would find in your parents' house, but Uncle Sam does not trust us with real babies but only tells us to try to learn all the ways to keep babies . . . well and good and happy. This is hard work and sometimes I feel a little discouraged. . . . Your letter cheers me up and I am glad you wrote, although I am obliged to send you this disappointing answer'" (Bradbury, *Five Decades of Action*, 7). An even more interesting example is found in Emily Abel, "A Document," *Journal of Women's History* 5 (Spring 1993): 83. The document is a long letter that initiated on-going correspondence between its writer and Julia Lathrop, who went so far as to try to find a better job for the writer's husband.

29. U.S. Children's Bureau, [*First*] *Annual Report* (Washington, D.C.: Government Printing Office, 1914), 84. Nancy P. Weiss found a letter from one woman

who put the situation graphically: "Now if your advice covers what an ordinary farm wife can carry out I would like to have it. Most of the advice I have read says—Fruite in plenty a bath every morning—gentle exercise . . . I have a perfectly fine husband a a loveing home but here is my day—get up at 5 A.M. hustle breakfast for 5, washin dishes help milk feed pigs clean up bakeing scrubbing washing (where is the gentle ex?) where could I have time for a bath every morn?" Nancy P. Weiss, "The Children's Bureau: A Case Study in Women's Voluntary Networks," presented at the Berkshire Conference, Bryn Mawr, Pa., June 10, 1976.

30. Lathrop, *Hull House Maps and Papers,* 143.

31. Julia Lathrop to Lillian Wald, Nov. 23, 1930, box 58, Abbott Papers, University of Chicago.

32. Jane Addams, *Democracy and Social Ethics* (New York: Macmillan, 1902), 221–77.

33. This story is well told in Costin, *Two Sisters,* 113–14.

34. U.S. Children's Bureau, [*Seventh*] *Annual Report* (Washington, D.C.: Government Printing Office, 1920), 725.

35. J. Stanley Lemons, *The Woman Citizen: Social Feminism in the 1920s* (Urbana: University of Illinois Press, 1973), 145–47. The Fair Labor Standards Act of 1938 embodied much of the agenda of the child labor reformers.

36. Happily, these letters, all from the spring of 1921, have been preserved in the voluminous Abbott Papers and in the Julia Lathrop Papers, Rockford College.

37. Louise M. Young, *In the Public Interest: The League of Women Voters, 1920–1970* (New York: Greenwood Press, 1989).

38. Costin, *Two Sisters,* 100.

39. Lemons, *The Woman Citizen,* 153–80.

40. A discussion of the phenomenon of women attacking other women appears in Kim Nielsen, *Un-American Womanhood: Anti-Radicalism, Anti-Feminism and the First Red Scare* (Columbus: Ohio State University Press, 2001).

41. Julia Lathrop to Katherine Lenroot, April 11, 1932, box 57, folder 1, Abbott Papers, University of Chicago.

42. Marian Wright Edelman, "The Shame of Child Poverty in the Richest Land on Earth," posting on Child Watch, the Children's Defense Fund Web-site, July 2002.

My Friend,
Julia Lathrop

Preface

When Grace Abbott and I undertook to write a life of Julia Clifford Lathrop we divided the writing along the lines of our most intimate experiences. So that it has come about that I have written the story of her life up to her appointment to the Children's Bureau in 1912.

Grace Abbott, her assistant and successor in the Bureau, who knows so intimately her brilliant administration during ten years in Washington, will cover that period and also her semi-official journeys in Europe with her services on the League of Nations Commission.

I again take up the story upon her return to Illinois for the last decade of her life.

It is said that biographers cannot hope to understand their subjects unless they breathe the same air. Grace Abbott can certainly claim this basis for understanding Julia Lathrop as few biographers can, and fortunately for me it has been taken care of by sheer juxtaposition of time and place. There was an almost striking similarity in the early experiences of Julia Lathrop and myself. We were born within two years of each other, in adjoining counties in northern Illinois. Both her father and mine had been active as Republicans in the political life of the region and both were characterized by the sturdy independence of the pioneer. Our friendship began before Hull-House opened, and developed through the years. I have found it difficult to avoid relating my own memories, and if at times I have not altogether succeeded in eliminating them I can only hope that they may prove illuminating to our shared experiences. Of one thing I am quite certain, that the brilliant

wit and understanding comments on life, so far as I have been able to
record them, are all hers.

—The Author

    After Miss Addams' death the manuscript for this book was found
to be practically ready for publication although she had not yet made
the final revision. It has fallen to me to do this and I have carried out
the task with scrupulous care, making as few changes as possible. The
book is therefore not quite as she would have made it but at least it
bears no imprint of any hand but her own.

—Alice Hamilton

1

Ancestry

When the subject of ancestry came up one day in a general conversation at Hull-House, Julia Lathrop almost pensively remarked that her first American ancestor would have come over in the Mayflower but for the unfortunate circumstance that he was in jail at the moment that doughty vessel set sail. When the laughter had somewhat subsided, a young resident who afterward became a judge of the supreme court in his state, commented: "That jail incident might be of great use to you in your daily sympathetic dealings with young criminals." She replied, "I have used it that way, and naturally the young criminals liked it, but as it was a little hard on the reverend gentleman I finally dropped it. It is a pity though to abandon a story that pleases both a soft-hearted criminal and a rising young lawyer who detests sentimentality."

The ancestor to whom Julia Lathrop referred was the Reverend John Lothropp who had received two degrees from Queen's College, Cambridge, and was settled as a "perpetual curate" at Edgton, Kent. "He had served his parish zealously for a number of years," when for conscience' sake he renounced holy orders and, uniting with the congregation of non-conformists that met in and about London, became their second minister. This congregation was tracked down to a house in Blackfriars by a pursuivant of Archbishop Laud, when Lothropp and two thirds of his congregation were arrested and the Pastor himself committed "to the clink." When he objected to being imprisoned there because the jail was not suitable for "a person of his high degree" the justice of his plea was recognized, and he was moved to another prison reserved for gentlemen, said to be the Tower of London. He was shown no further leniency by the Archbishop, but at the end of two years he appealed directly to the King and his petition "for liberty to go in exile" was granted in April, 1624.

He did not go in exile too promptly however for it was more than ten years later when he accepted an invitation from the settlers of Scituate, in the Colony of New Plymouth to become their pastor. His wife had died during his imprisonment leaving him the care of eight children, six of whom, four sons and two daughters, he took to America with him. Governor Winslow recorded his arrival with his thirty followers at Boston, in the good ship *Griffin,* September 18, 1634. Upon landing, John Lothropp proceeded immediately to Scituate, arriving on a Saturday night and preaching twice the following day. In Scituate he married a second wife, a widow, whom he mentions affectionately but all too briefly as Anne. According to one chronicler they had six children; according to another there were only two sons, Barnabas and John, but perhaps four daughters were pushed so far into the background that they disappeared from the record. There is an unsubstantiated tradition that because John Lothropp and his congregation were less orthodox than the Mayflower Puritans, they removed from Scituate to Barnstable, which was not so near to the seat of Puritan orthodoxy. At any rate they went there in 1639 and there John Lothropp remained until his death six years later, when he was universally acclaimed "a sound scholar and a lively preacher." One enthusiastic chronicler states that John Lothropp "heads the list of the Godly and able Gospel preachers who adorned the Colony and gave light in a resplendent and glorious manner."

All of John Lothropp's children founded families in New England, but a clue of descent is afforded by the spelling of the name. Lathrop, sometimes spelled Laythrop, which represents the New England pronunciation of Lathrop, was adopted by the descendants of the same family, while the others wrote the name Lothropp.

Under one or another spelling, they all remained in New England until Julia Lathrop's great-grandfather, Adgate Lathrop, removed to western New York. The family lived on a large farm in Genesee County, and it was there John Lathrop, Julia's grandfather, married Martha Clifford. There were two sons in the family, William and Whitman, the elder of whom, born April 4, 1825, was Julia Lathrop's father. Of the four daughters, Mary the oldest, who married a farmer named Benham, was an exceptionally fine teacher, held in high esteem by her fellow citizens; Anne, considered the handsomest member of the family, married Dr. C. James Taggart, a young physician who settled in Rockford, Illinois. She was a favorite sister of Julia Lathrop's father and was always known in his household as Auntie Taggart. The third daughter, Julia, died when she was very little. There was a tradition that once, when this early Julia Lathrop was put into a flower pot and brought from the garden into the house, her mother impulsively exclaimed that she was the prettiest plant that such a pot could ever hold. The youngest child was Martha Clifford, "Aunt Mat" to Julia Lathrop's family, who was a missionary in India for many years. The mother of the John Lathrop family died when Martha was born, and the baby went to live with her grandparents. In later life, Martha recalled, with that vividness with which a child always remembers the trappings of death, that when her grandfather died, the grave could not be dug because the snow was too deep, so that the body was kept in a cold room until warmer weather came, and that his wife used to go in and see him every day.

John Lathrop married a second wife, Elizabeth Moss, and there was another set of children. It may have been the inevitable stepmother attitude, but as a devout member of the Episcopal church she achieved what Archbishop Laud was unable to do, "made the church very unpopular in the family."

William Lathrop, Julia's father, attended an academy at Lima, New York, for parts of several years and later read law with a lawyer in Attica. He was very restless on the farm and left Genesee County in 1849, going to Rockford, Illinois, where his Aunt Adeline Lathrop, a daughter of Adgate Lathrop who had married a Presbyterian minister, Joel Potter, was then living.

William Lathrop hoped to begin at once the practice of law in Rockford but found it difficult and, like all the young men who followed Horace Greeley's advice to "go West," he looked about him before he determined on his ultimate location. He visited two brothers of his mother, the Cliffords, who were railroad contractors south of Rockford, but he could earn only two dollars a day working for these uncles and he pursued his investigation of Illinois towns further south and west. The following letter from William Lathrop to his aunt, Adeline Lathrop Potter, described his trip to New Albany, and revealed that his mind was already turning to Rockford for his ultimate location, for although he was admitted to the bar at Knoxville, Illinois, in 1850, he returned to Rockford the next year.

Knoxville, Knox Co., Ill., May 9th, 1850

Dear Aunt,

Perhaps after my positive promise on leaving your place this delay may have caused some surprise but it has not been because I have either forgotten you or the kindness with which I was received. I had a very pleasant ride and arrived here on the Friday morning following. We followed the river bank nearly all the way to Dixon and I must say I was delighted with the scenery between Byron and Dixon. In variety and beauty it far surpasses the broad plain of Rockford. Many of the rocky piles and abrupt bluffs would lose nothing by comparison with more celebrated localities. From Dixon we went directly to New Albany on the Mississippi some thirty-five miles above Rock Island. I had a very fine view of the river which I had always felt curious to behold as the road to the latter place lay along the bank except where it was overflown and here in many places I thought it lay far out in the stream. From Rock Island to Monmouth the country is very sparsely settled but had I been in New York I should have been constantly on the lookout for dwellings. These old looking fields without an occupant have not entirely lost their novelty for me.

One thing I could not help observing, that from Rockford on that section of country every step south gave indications of a less enterprising community. The soil seems to be of surpassing fertility and perhaps this fact together with the remoteness of a market accounts for the indolence of the people. But I fear the customs of the land of their birth has more influence upon their habits than the circumstances with which they are surrounded. Some individual farmers in this section are exceptions to the general rule and are accumulating property with unparalleled rapidity. Could these rich prairies pass into the hands of Eastern people with all their commercial facilities a few years would serve to put this state upon a financial footing which a half century will fail to do under the present state of affairs. I believe this part of the state, naturally rich

as it is, is shunned by the better class of Eastern Settlers. Those that
have known and enjoyed the advantages of quick returns for labor
are loth to hopelessly exclude themselves from them. I can think of
no other reason why Wisconsin and Northern Illinois are more
rapidly filling up than this part of the state except the brighter
prospects that the resources of those sections are sooner to be developed. From what I have seen and can learn I think this portion
of the state is equally as well, if not better, adapted to the growth
of grain as it is further north. Timber is more plenty and of a better quality here than about Rockford. The trees are larger and taller
and look more like an Eastern growth. I am better pleased with the
country than I expected to be when I left your place. The country
was not fairly represented by some of the gentlemen who assumed
to be well acquainted here. This village looks old in comparison
with yours. The buildings are not of the first order and many of
them old and rusty at that. The Locust planted for shade trees appear nearly as old as those of Western N.Y., but fruit trees with the
exception of peaches are small and few for a country as long settled as this. Knoxville might be a place of some importance and
possibly yet may be. The presence of a few enterprising men with
capital here would give the place a new aspect. We have no water
power, but there is no place where steam power could be used to
better advantage or obtained at less cost. Coal is abundant and very
cheap. The place feels the want of a produce market and its absence
is driving trade of all kinds into less important channels. For mills
we have nothing but one old steam shell, the merest apology I ever
saw for a mill, and one driven by horse power. These defects may
yet be remedied but I confess I see no immediate prospect. The
people seem too well satisfied with their present condition and the
efforts which some of the surrounding places are making render
still more difficult the task of restoring to the place the importance
which it deserves from its locality.

I think, if I live, of remaining here till fall and may longer, but
my favorable impressions of the North are by no means removed.
I have written to Lewis and I think as earnestly as you requested
that he should visit you. I have not heard from home yet. Business
prospects are not quite so flattering as I had hoped. I may yet con-
clude to go north and work on a farm. Aunt, I hardly anticipate
that I can write in any way interesting to you, I am surrounded with

no circumstances to make it so, but I should be very glad to hear from you and Uncle at all times.

Yours sincerely,

WILLIAM LATHROP.

A. L. Potter.

William Lathrop avoided the opportunities for speculation which the new country afforded. He was serious and hard working perhaps because he remembered that his father, a prosperous farmer, had lost his property on a power venture believing that he could develop a stream on his farm to supply power for factories.

He returned to Rockford in 1851 and the next year participated in the incorporation of the village into a city. At the first meeting of the Council, he was appointed City Clerk and at the second meeting was made City Attorney, holding both offices through the first years of the municipality's life. These offices were for him but the beginning of a long line of public spirited activities for the city of Rockford, for the state and for the nation. The village had at first been called "Midway," as halfway between Galena and Chicago on a line of four-horse coaches, but because the Indians had found the water in the Rock River so shallow at one point as to be easily forded by their ponies, the name of Rockford was finally adopted in the first city charter.

Julia Lathrop's mother, Adeline Potter Lathrop, was a daughter of Eleazer Hubbell Potter, one of eight brothers. Eleazer Potter came to Rockford from Medina, New York, in 1837, with his wife Adeline Eells Potter and their two children, Edward Eells Potter, three years old, and Sarah Adeline Potter, Julia's mother, one year old. Mr. Potter's partner, a man named Preston, came with him bringing his wife and three little girls. The newcomers reached the settlement on Rock River at the mouth of Kent Creek which had been established three years earlier by Germanicus Kent and Thatcher Blake, who, when they were investigating the quickly acquired fortunes of the Galena lead miners, had been told of the beauties of the Rock River country by a soldier returning from the Black Hawk War. The two men had set out from Galena in the spring of 1834, in a democrat wagon loaded with a canoe designed to bring them down the Rock River. They were delighted with the region and having entered their claims, proceeded to build a dam along the Rock River and to erect a sawmill.

In this little settlement which by 1837 was already becoming a center of a growing farm district, the newcomers opened a general store, Preston & Potter, which prospered from the start and grew with the town.

The story of those early days told by Julia's mother concerned the ford of Rock River for which the town was named. She remembered when as a little girl she was crossing the river with her parents that she was jounced out of the buggy when it hit a rock. Perhaps this incident increased her father's zeal for a bridge to replace the ford for he worked very hard to have one built. When such a bridge was about to be completed, to show his pleasure in the accomplishment, he rode across when the first span was still unfloored, waving his hat to his friends on the other side.

The Potters brought with them from New York a beautiful grandfather's clock which they carried on the bottom of the wagon. On the face of the clock was "Edward Eells, Middlebury, Vt." He was the father of Adeline Eells Potter, a sea captain, who according to family tradition made not only the clock but also the cabinet work on the beautiful inlaid case.

Adeline Eells Potter died in 1838, and Mr. Potter, who went to New York City twice a year to purchase stock for his flourishing business, returned from one of these journeys with a bride, Mary Morrell, who had been born and reared in New York City and whose orthodox family was identified with the old Brick Presbyterian Church. She happily joined the Congregationalists, who had voted to combine with the Presbyterians to found the first of the Rockford churches. The Potters were well known for their piety, among the many New England families who had come to Rockford, some of them by way of western New York. There was a second family of Potter children, Andrew, George and Mary, who was always called "Aunt Kit" by the Lathrop family.

Eleazer Potter was a black-eyed handsome man, although his brother Henry was considered the handsomest, as he was the tallest, of the eight Potter brothers. Henry with his brother Mark, who also studied law, went to Texas where they became southern in sentiment and the family never knew what became of them as the Civil War broke off all communications. Like many another divided family in that tragic period, they could only hope that the separated kinsfolk would not be brought actually face to face in battle.

Commodore Edward Eells Potter, Julia's uncle, graduated from Annapolis and served in the Navy throughout the Civil War, much of the time on a gunboat on the Mississippi. The Commodore was a handsome and dashing man with high standards of personal and professional conduct. He continued in the Navy after the war and was long gratefully remembered by the seamen because he had insisted that the sailors should be given coffee in the early morning before they swabbed down the deck.

Rockford grew rapidly during the fifties and sixties, and the following description written by an early citizen is characterized by the exuberant good will of the pioneers: "Society was free from artificial distinctions and amusements were instructive as well as entertaining. Public balls, popular among a class of residents, were usually held at one of the new hotels. Christmas and New Years were the favorite dates. Literary entertainments were occasionally given at the courthouse, weddings were the large social gatherings, and the invitations were quite general."

Bayard Taylor in a letter to the *New York Tribune* published as early as the spring of 1855 paid Rockford this generous tribute: "I last wrote to you from Rockford, the most beautiful town in northern Illinois. It has the advantage of an admirable waterpower furnished by the Rock River; of a rich, rolling prairie which is fast being settled and farmed on all sides; of a fine building material in its quarries of soft yellow limestone resembling the Roman travertine, and of an unusually enterprising and intelligent population. . . . I was pleased to note that taste keeps pace with prosperity." He somewhat patronizingly concludes: "The grounds of the very fine specimens of home architecture are admirably laid out; there is nothing better of the kind on the Hudson." In one of the houses so approved, the Potter family of which Julia Lathrop's mother was the oldest daughter, resided for many years.

Eleazer Hubbell Potter, Julia's grandfather, as a prosperous man in early Rockford was able to secure the best educational advantages for his children that the vicinity afforded. His eldest son Edward was sent from the Rockford public schools to the newly established academy at

Mt. Morris, Illinois, and Adeline, Julia's mother, entered and graduated with the first class at Rockford Female Seminary. This early educational institution, long known by its original name but for many years since as Rockford College, was founded by Congregational clergymen and laymen of the Northwest in June 1849. At the same time they established a college for men at a safe distance up the Rock River in Beloit, Wisconsin. Anna P. Sill was the first principal of the Seminary and remained in charge of the growing institution for many years. The first class which entered in 1851 numbered fifteen students and Adeline Potter was its youngest member. She was a second year student in July 1852 when the cornerstone of the first building, Middle Hall, was laid by the Rev. Aratus Kent of Galena who preached a widely admired sermon upon the text, "That our daughters may be as corner stones polished after the similitude of a palace."

Adeline Potter graduated with the first class in 1854. This happy event is described by a professor from Beloit College from whom we quote:

> On the 13th of July, with high anticipation and glad that another year's labors were ended, we left "La Belle City" of Beloit, to witness our "Alma Soror" at Rockford, crowned with honors by the first graduating class. Dame Nature for the most part seemed to smile for the joyous occasion. . . . The audience was assembled in the chapel, which occupies the third story of the beautiful seminary building. The walls of the chapel were embellished with paintings and the ceiling adorned with fair gifts of summer, but the chief charm of all was that host of the daughters of Beauty and their galaxy of laughing eyes. . . . The exercises of the afternoon consisted of an address by Prof. Emerson of Beloit College, the Valedictory by Miss Adeline Potter and the giving of diplomas.
>
> Prof. Emerson's address was characteristic of the man, original, forceful and abounding in passages of classic beauty. The valedictory was very interesting and attentively listened to. To us one of the chief beauties was that through it all was poured the grateful spirit of woman's gentler nature. A few extracts will be more complimentary than any comments we can make. In speaking of the founders of the institution which was now about to graduate its first class, the valedictorian says:

"They saw the daughters of the prairied west thirsty for cooling draughts from learning's spring—then their hearts were filled with true compassion and they soon unsealed *this* crystal fountain. We had quaffed the soul inspiring cup as we took it dripping from the sparkling waters, and often as we drank, we thanked the giver of the blessing, but to-day our hearts are welling up anew with gratitude and our souls are full, *too* full of thankfulness to express the *half* we feel, yet their memory will be held most precious, remembered with the unforgotten treasures of the past."

Here is a tribute to the honored principal of the seminary:

"'Tis she who has ever gone before us, been our friend, our counsellor and guide, she has opened stores of knowledge that before we knew not to exist—she has awakened in our souls those latent feelings, roused unformed desires that impelled us to go forward in the search for hidden truths, when perhaps we should have fainted and fallen in the way by the weight of trials that we met. . . ."

The parting word is truly beautiful:

"Woman's lot is on us now and it is hers to scatter richest flowers in the pathway to Heaven, to remove the hidden thorn and place a wreath of roses in its stead; and we must leave you now to perform her silent mission.

"Though widely may our paths of life diverge, yet if all point toward the Celestial City, we may meet at last around the Saviour's throne, each with the jewels she has brought to gem his crown."

I recall Adeline Potter Lathrop very vividly at the fiftieth anniversary of the first class which graduated from Rockford College, my own alma mater. There had been seven members, fifty years before and they were all alive and all there—an exhibition of longevity which the life insurance men declared to be phenomenal. As they forgathered, the missionaries, the teachers and housewives, most of them were accompanied by children or grandchildren, although each one asserted she would have been quite able to come alone. Three of the early graduates whom I had long known remain clearly in my memory as they appeared that day. One was Caroline Potter Brazee, my old teacher in literature. The hours spent with her in "critical readings," as she called them, were not quite class work nor quite recreation, but those readings after the lapse of more than fifty years, are still surrounded with a sort of enchantment, first evoked I think by Milton's "Comus." Another friend was her cousin, Julia Lathrop's mother, who had been most kind to me during my years in Rockford College, and a third friend was Elizabeth Griffin Abbott, the mother of Grace Abbott, Julia Lathrop's successor in the Children's Bureau and at that time her assistant.

It was a matter of pride to the college that the mothers of the chief and the assistant chief of the Children's Bureau were members of the early classes of Rockford Seminary. The two mothers themselves were rather amused at the flowery references the Commencement orators made to the coincidence and remarked that it was an honor to the college only because the girls had done their work well and, good suffragists as they both were, they added: but after all what was more natural than that women should take charge of the work for children when the Federal Government finally decided to pay attention to them as well as to the progeny of fish and to the calves and little pigs which, so far as the young were concerned, had up to then monopolized its interest?

William Lathrop was a staunch Republican from the beginning. In 1854 he was one of forty-six citizens to sign a call for a meeting to organize the Republican party in northern Illinois. In 1856 he was elected a member of the first Republican Legislature of Illinois. He ordered a new coat for the Legislature, which came home lined with white satin, the tailor having assumed that it was for his rumored wedding for which white satin was considered most appropriate.

It was during his legislative term at Springfield that he first saw Abraham Lincoln. Mr. Lathrop who had been reading in the State Library was hunting for a book when he saw a man sitting with his feet up forming a long triangle. The ungainly man brought his chair down to ask if he could help find anything, and between them the book was quickly secured. Mr. Lathrop never amplified the story but the simple recital always thrilled his hearers whenever he could be induced to tell it.

By 1857 William Lathrop, well established in the practice of law, had saved $10,000—that first ten thousand which all self-made men agree is the hardest to accumulate and which sometimes represents such severe self-denial that it results in an incapacity for later enjoyment of money itself. He had worked hard not only because economic independence had become a great objective to him, but because for two years he had been engaged to marry Joel Potter's niece and was anxious to establish a home of his own.

In June, 1857, William Lathrop and Sarah Adeline Potter were married and for their wedding trip they went by boat to St. Paul, Minnesota, at that time a very fashionable journey. The Mississippi River was then full of steamboats plying between St. Paul and New Orleans. They doubtless journeyed on one of the famous side-wheelers magnificently called "floating palaces." As recently portrayed by Janet Fairbank in *Bright Land* the chimneys of such a steamboat rose sixty feet into the air; her railings, the corners of her pilot house and the roof of her hurricane deck were all outlined in filigree carving; her paddle boxes were gaily decorated; flags flew from her flagpole and a Negro string orchestra played on her guards as the passengers hurried aboard. Nowhere else on the American Continent at that moment was there so much water traffic so brilliantly bedizened. As the steamboat approached Galena, the citizens of which had been so closely identified with earliest Rockford, they must have seen a levee of bewildering activity; innumerable pigs of lead were piled into the packets, and from the boats were unloaded all manner of necessities for the vast country to the west of the great river. Galena was the main outfitting point for the pioneer settlers further west and for the forts maintained by the government in hostile Indian country.

By hearsay I was more or less familiar with Galena from my earliest childhood because for sixteen years my father represented in the Illinois Senate Jo Daviess County in which that town is situated. Galena was one of the places through which Illinois had become involved in the growth of the new Northwest and in the development of transcontinental projects in which state legislation played its part.

2

The Lathrop Family
in Northern Illinois

🐟 Shortly after the return from the wedding journey to St. Paul Mr. Lathrop bought a corner lot on the west side of the river although the growing town was at that moment on the east side. Native oak trees were scattered over the lot but he supplemented by planting elms, repeating the planting three times before the trees grew although he watered them every night on his return from the office, pumping all the water which he carried pailful by pailful. The lot had a house on it in which the family lived during the first winter, planning to build a new house in the spring. Mrs. Lathrop's father, however, who had been not only a successful merchant but president of the largest bank of the town, suffered disaster in the financial panic during the autumn of 1857—the very year of the Lathrops' marriage. Up to that date everything had been going prosperously for the little town and the pioneers and Mr. Potter had built a large stone house only a few blocks away from the corner lot newly purchased by the Lathrops. After the disaster the young couple postponed building a new house and lived in the little house already there. In this house five children were born: Julia Clifford, on June 29, 1858, Anna Hubbell, Edward Potter and later William Taggart and Robert, the two latter long known in the family as the "little boys." Mr. Lathrop finally built a house on Rockford Avenue, of Milwaukee cream brick, which became the permanent family home.

William Lathrop was very active as a lawyer and his practice took him into all the counties of northern Illinois. Julia as a little girl used to hear him speak of having suits in one town or another and she always wondered why he did not bring them home and let the family see him

wear them. He was a good lawyer, completely wrapped up in his profession and as one of the distinguished lawyers in the state of Illinois he
was defense lawyer in some of the most famous murder cases ever tried
in the northern half of the state, among them one in the sixties known
as the "Dixon case," in which he defended a woman who had shot her
husband because she believed that he intended to steal the baby from
her. This was the first case in Illinois where emotional insanity was the
defense. Mr. Lathrop secured the acquittal of the mother of the baby.
There were naturally many stories in Rockford concerning his wit and
wisdom. Among them was one related of Will Butterworth who was
running the gasworks in Rockford when John Sherratt was Mayor. In a
controversy about a contract for lighting the streets of Rockford Mr.
Butterworth wrote a very angry letter to the Mayor, but happily he
showed it to his attorney William Lathrop before he sent it. The latter
took the letter, read it through and then put it in his desk and shut the
drawer. He said to Mr. Butterworth "Come back here at eight o'clock
in the morning; I want to talk to you then." Mr. Butterworth came back
the next morning and Mr. Lathrop said "Butterworth, for God's sake
never write a letter when you're mad"—"The best piece of advice a
lawyer ever gave me," said his client years afterwards.

Mr. Lathrop was a very good extemporaneous speaker and only occasionally wrote his speeches. He had a flashing wit and the ability suddenly to give a brilliant turn to the situation under discussion. His opponents learned to dread the effect upon a jury of his compelling eyes.
His daughter Julia was very like him in her quick and spontaneous wit.
Although Mr. Lathrop was a hard-working, serious man, when he
would permit himself light conversation he could be very amusing, in
which accomplishment Julia again was very like him. I served on a
board with Mr. Lathrop as a trustee of Rockford College during a period of financial distress when he alone was able to break through our
gloom and fill the trustees' room with unexpected laughter.

Julia's mother, Adeline Potter Lathrop, was a good student all her
life and a reader of worth while books. Despite the fact that she was occupied with household interests and the care of active children, with
some other Rockford women she formed the Monday Club. The Club
met Monday afternoons to read and discuss books but wrote no papers

themselves, saying frankly that they preferred to read matter written by people who knew how to write better than they did. Mrs. Lathrop was very active in the Second Congregational Church. She was an ardent suffragist and as she and her husband had strong convictions about the rights of women, the two older children were never put at a disadvantage because they were girls. There was always a free atmosphere in the home where all of the children freely expressed their opinions and were encouraged to work out their own interests without parental interference. Although Mr. Lathrop disapproved of extravagance and "did not believe in trying every new thing" he was always very liberal in regard to books and the children were allowed to buy all they needed with the sympathetic understanding of their parents.

In the early days William Lathrop sent for his youngest sister Martha who lived in his home while she attended Rockford Seminary. She graduated there before she went to India as a missionary under the auspices of the Women's Union Missionary Society in New York.

Several distinguished men in northern Illinois were well known for their liberality in religious belief, although during every political campaign in which they were involved, they were roundly denounced by the local preachers following the example of the circuit rider, Peter Cartwright, who had so brilliantly heckled Abraham Lincoln on his religion during his campaign for Congress. Mr. Lathrop held to his liberal beliefs in religious matters although he never used the cheap arguments of the village atheist nor the telling phrases of Robert Ingersoll who was then proclaiming "the mistakes of Moses" throughout the country.

Mr. Lathrop was so respectful of his wife's beliefs that he went to church quite regularly in the rôle of *pater familias* and the children were sent to Sunday School although it is rumored the boys often demurred. Mrs. Lathrop sometimes regretted that theirs was the only Potter household in Rockford that did not have family prayers, but her husband could not help her there and in any case he declared that he considered going to church for the sake of an example to a family a mighty poor substitute for piety. When none of the children, in spite of their mother's hopes for them, ever became church members at the age considered proper for such a step, he whimsically declared that he would attend church no more for his painfully achieved example had been a failure.

It may have been partly due to that "incessant suggestion of change which always went with pioneer life" that Mr. Lathrop like others of the early comers to Illinois was very liberal in his views in regard to women's place in society. He felt very strongly that women ought not to be held back by legal restrictions; that they should have responsibilities and be prepared to meet them. There may have been other reasons for his belief that woman's "sphere" should be enlarged. As a member of the Illinois Legislature he may easily have been present when Susan B. Anthony came before it as she did many times to advocate equal rights for women, or he may have heard the older men tell of Dorothy Dix when she came by wagon to Springfield from Chicago in the forties to plead with the representatives of the people of Illinois for humane treatment for the insane and secured the passage of a law authorizing the first asylum for the insane in the state. Those early Republicans who in time came to advocate the overthrow of slavery were filled with gratitude to Harriet Beecher Stowe for the popular backing she had so tremendously created for their cause. William Lathrop lived up to his beliefs in this as in other respects. The first woman lawyer in Illinois, Alta Hulett, read law in his office and he drew the bill permitting women in Illinois to be admitted to the bar. In his belief that women should have equal opportunities with men he was very liberal in regard to his daughters' activities. Julia had no great ambition in which she was thwarted although many a young woman of that period did not share her experience.

Of course the great moral and political issue which overshadowed everything else in the 1850's was the limitation of slavery and later its total abolition on American soil. It is curious how children catch the glow of the moral enthusiasm of their elders and absorb opinions by listening even though the issue touches them most remotely. Many children belonging to abolitionist families as Julia Lathrop did and as I did, knew vaguely of grave matters which were being discussed over their heads. I must have been less than four years old when I saw a slave, but I have never forgotten the black man sitting in quiet conversation with my father as I entered a room one sunny morning. He was being helped to Canada where he would become free, and how valiantly I prayed that he would have a safe journey. I was of course told not to talk about him, and although I would sometimes whisper an inquiry into my father's ear he never could tell me the outcome of the slave's desperate effort for freedom.

The public debate so brilliantly carried on by Lincoln and Douglas throughout the state of Illinois gave Lincoln a hearing, as he himself said, on the great enduring questions of the age and he used the opportunity to plead for civil liberty with that tremendous power of his to penetrate to fundamental principles. Many of his fellow citizens to whom the spoken word was still the living word were laid under a lasting moral compunction. This discussion was by no means purely academic. My father as a state senator was one of a number of legislators who one day went to St. Louis, outside of the jurisdiction of the state of Illinois, so that there might be no quorum to take a vote on the secession of the state from the Union—a vote for which the members of the southern end of the state had carefully prepared. The lower end of Illinois had been settled by migrants from the South, whose natural avenue of approach was the Mississippi River and its tributaries including the Illinois River. The members of the Legislature knew of the difficulties all about them ever since 1837 when Elijah Lovejoy was killed at Alton, Illinois, and his abolition press destroyed for the fourth time.

Springfield at that moment was full of men who afterwards became national figures. In addition to Lincoln himself and the two men later so identified with him in the White House, John Hay and John G. Nicolay, were Stephen Douglas, Lyman Trumbull, Judge Davis and others. An historian has lately written that "Fate summoned Illinois to play a critical part in the crisis which had been preparing since the foundation of their country."

During all these pioneer years there was a growing tendency throughout the country to hold the "foreigners" as the immigrants were called who had been coming in increasing numbers since 1830, in contemptuous contrast to freeborn American citizens. An incident in Rockford may have tended to increase this attitude throughout the community. In its early days the North Western Railway had dropped off a load of Swedish immigrants, sick and dying with what was believed to be cholera. Col.

Marsh turned his barn over to them, the well taking care of the sick, and Mrs. Marsh, a connection of the Lathrop family, supplied them with food and nursing equipment. She was vigilant in keeping the Swedes within the barn and all the neighborhood children away from the barn. The Swedish survivors who settled in Rockford have added ever since to their numbers and have become prosperous citizens, but for years they with all other immigrants doubtless vaguely realized the attitude of many Americans toward immigrants as such, although the tradition obtains that Mr. Lathrop once said that the Scandinavians were the making of Rockford. An aloofness to immigrants was in marked contrast to the general good will of the pioneers toward each other. Perhaps the patriotic Americans were a little afraid of being overwhelmed by newcomers who might sweep away their carefully accumulated gains in free government. At any rate, to this very day an excessive patriotism tends to show itself in a criticism of the foreign born and in a suspicion of his political views. It was all the more remarkable therefore that Julia Lathrop, whose childhood must have reflected this community attitude, should later have developed such an unusual understanding of immigrants and their problems.

In one respect, Julia Lathrop continued and carried on the same cause to which her father had been devoted. William Lathrop even in the earliest periods of its agitation was an ardent advocate of civil service reform and in the general election of 1876, when it had become the subject of widespread political discussion, he was elected to Congress on a platform pledging him to its advocacy. During all of his service as a representative in Congress he was an unswerving supporter of measures designed to eliminate bossism from public service. When it was his right as a member of Congress to nominate a Rockford postmaster he declined to do so and referred the matter to a vote of the people, resulting in the choice of Col. Lawler. Such an act of sterling worth might be designated as a throw-back into our early American idealism or the promise of a fairer day in our national self-government. Certainly it was absolutely revolutionary in politics at a moment when the spoils as a matter of course belonged to the victor. Mr. Lathrop was one of the first congressmen to appoint a cadet to West Point on the ground of fitness ascertained by a competitive examination, following his lifelong habit of backing up his convictions by action.

Illinois was not unlike the other states in the combination of political and commercial corruption relating to public funds. In 1876 many men were in office who had been elected solely upon their Civil War records without regard to their fitness to perform official duties. That offices should be filled in relation to party activity was almost automatic. So noisome had this general corruption become that as late as 1890 Theodore Roosevelt became a civil service commissioner in Washington because he believed that such a post afforded the highest type of service to be rendered to his country by a citizen of courage and public spirit. In her efforts for civil service reform, Julia Lathrop followed her father's splendid initiative. She too translated her convictions into actions throughout her years as an official in county, state and nation.

When Mr. Lathrop came to Rockford in 1851, it was a small town with court house and church and general store and it was not until the early sixties when machine industry began to invade the Mississippi Valley, that Rockford gradually became a manufacturing center. The earliest large industries were in agricultural implements in which several fortunes were made and lost in Rockford owing largely to difficulties about patents.

I recall that during the ten years when Rockford College generously gave Hull-House the use of its buildings for a summer school, the faculty and students very much enjoyed the hospitality of what remained of a fine estate on a little bluff now incorporated into the city. A manufacturer of agricultural implements long before had built an imposing mansion for winter use, a Swiss cottage approached by a suspension bridge over the ravine for summer. Both houses were filled with what were then called souvenirs of European travel.

In considering the social trend in northern Illinois it must be remembered that these early citizens of the Middle West had witnessed the boom of railroad building and later the heyday of industrial development under the economic theory of *laissez faire* which at that moment ruled the English speaking world and protected the business man from "interference" by either industrial or fiscal legislation. The manufacturing interests in Rockford grew rapidly and like the industries in Chicago and elsewhere attained gigantic proportions during the last third of the nineteenth century. The manufacturers claimed and received the adulation of the entire population so dependent upon their good will. As the pioneers gave the railroads everything they wanted because the development of the country pivoted upon their services, so they enthusiastically cherished the first huge industries. To criticise them was considered unpatriotic. They were especially popular in the eighties, for in that decade the manufacturing interests of the region had already begun the tremendous drive which by 1930 had shifted the manufacturing center for the entire nation from the Atlantic coast to one of the southeastern suburbs of Chicago. It was perhaps inevitable under such circumstances that the organized working men with their demands for higher wages, backed by an occasional strike or threat of one, constantly tended to be regarded as inimical to the best interests of the community and were easily blamed for every industrial and commercial set-back.

Whatever Julia Lathrop's early impressions in a "high tariff man-ufacturing city" may have been, her sympathetic knowledge of this at-titude proved of value in that great art of understanding life in which she was so proficient.

3

Childhood and Vassar College, 1858–1880

๛ To return to Julia Lathrop's childhood itself, which after all concerns us more than the social implications of her early surroundings however important to later life the conditions in childhood may be— Julia went to the public school where she was always reported a "good child" and a "smart scholar." She was, however, timid and shy and to the end of her life felt strongly that children are often treated with entire lack of respect and without understanding. She once told of an incident which occurred when she was about seven years old. The teacher in her schoolroom had a custom of sometimes sending a note to a teacher in a boys' room upstairs and as the selection of the little girls to perform this service was based on good behavior and correct lessons most of them liked it. One day the teacher having selected Julia for the errand bade her come to her desk to get the note. Julia Lathrop in telling the story said that before her mind arose the stairs, the long corridors, and worst of all, the passage between the lines of boys to the teacher's desk and it seemed to her that she would much rather die than encounter all these terrors. She therefore steadily shook her head which was all she could do as her mouth was dry and the power of speech had deserted her. The teacher continued to urge her and at last said, "Julia Lathrop, you are as stubborn as a mule!" The ungracious remark deeply distressed the little girl and doubtless afforded amusement to her small classmates who heard it but although she felt dimly outraged she said it was years before she realized how abominably she had been treated.

There was for many children during the sixties a consciousness of the Civil War intensified in Julia Lathrop's case by stories of her young uncle Andrew Potter, who served in the 74th Illinois Regiment. He was a gallant soldier who "did not know what fear was," and his possible fate must have filled her with constant apprehension. Of course there are many stories of her unending kindness to man and beast. One of her brothers tells that a family horse, Old Bill, once stepped upon a bolt which induced lockjaw, to the great concern of all of them. When the brother went to administer a dose of medicine at midnight he found Julia sitting beside Old Bill in his box stall, which was illuminated by a student's lamp she had brought with her. In response to his astonished inquiry, "What are you doing here?"—she said that Old Bill was not quite so lonesome when somebody was in the stall with him.

There is also the story of her efforts to feed a pet calf on the fresh grass of the side lawn. Although the calf pulled mercilessly on the other end of the rope she was holding, she did not mind it so long as he was finding a new lush place for his eating, but when he pulled "from meanness," she admitted that the rope skinned her hands.

She always ran away from school as hard as she could if it was rumored that a boy was to be flogged after school hours, and when one of her brothers, while he was still young enough to be put across the principal's knee, managed to bite the leg of his chastiser, to his pleased surprise Julia laid aside her rôle of older sister and evinced a wicked satisfaction in the achievement.

Another brother tells that when he was ten years old and Julia seemed to him quite grown up, he broke a school rule in regard to snowballing and that the illegal ball not only flew in the wrong direction but struck the school principal squarely in the middle of the back. The principal who was very angry, told the boy to go home and stay there, leaving him uncertain whether he was suspended, expelled or merely in for a disciplinary beating from the principal himself. His father's comment was "What happens next seems to be your own affair," but Julia took him back to school,—his pride was so far reduced that he was even willing to take her hand,—and achieved one of her early diplomatic adjustments by getting something of an apology from the boy and something of a concession from the irate principal.

There is a widespread tradition that she was very inventive in regard to amateur dramatics and often made up plays for the younger children. While she kept the youngsters enormously entertained, like a good

impresario she was stern as to their conduct on the stage. When a bud-
ding genius once complained that he was not acting at the moment of
reproof, only being himself, and therefore was not subject to stage rules,
she sternly replied, "Bad behavior is worse than bad acting." It may have
been on one such occasion that a small brother remarked, "You are not
a mother to us as the oldest sister ought to be; you are a perfect stepmother to us. Father had a real one and so did mother, and that sure is
enough for the entire family!" Perhaps Rockford children were easily
interested in dramatics; at any rate they all knew the story that in 1838
when Joe Jefferson was a youth acting Lord Lovell in his father's theatrical company, while en route from Chicago to Galena he was weather
bound in Rockford where the children knew he had to stay for a long
time. Owing to this incident one set of children after another claimed
to have seen Joe Jefferson in Rip Van Winkle with a personal sense of
proprietorship and it was a favorite pastime in a group of children for
each to describe how the dog Schneider had looked when he was seen
upon the stage. To some he was black and small and to others spotted
and large, but the joke at the end was always the same, that there had
never really been a dog of any sort on the stage, that Joe Jefferson had
only made everybody believe there was. Many of the children remained
forever unconvinced and argued with each other interminably.

There is a story among the older people in Rockford that in an English play given by the Argonauts, Julia Lathrop walked away with the
house in a scene in which as a slavey she blacked boots in such an en-
gaging manner that she was loudly recalled but she became so confused
by the applause following her reappearance that she tried to break
through a piece of scenery in her effort to escape and was rescued with
some difficulty from the ensuing jam. Such innocent tales of the stage
were not allowed to make dramatics too tame for there was always
Shakespeare full of murders and accusing ghosts, of which Julia Lathrop as dramatic director often availed herself. In fact I recall years later
when I was a student at Rockford College that we begged Julia Lathrop
who had just returned from Vassar to come over and help us with the
witches' scene from Macbeth which we were incorporating into a Wal-
purgis night celebration. The scene was quite beyond our amateur ability and possibly also of hers although we were much impressed by the
vigor and originality with which she tackled our problem and trium-

phantly pulled off the performance. With all the other girls at Rockford College I greatly admired this brilliant young woman who came from a real woman's college carrying her honors with such a quick wit and disarming charm as to fairly put to rout our heavy ideas of higher education for women.

The children had their household tasks to perform which Julia always stood up to although she never developed a special interest in housework. To the end of her life however she had an unusual gift for what is sometimes termed household decoration. In later years she was famous for a very good omelette, and it was a gala Sunday supper at Hull-House when she consented to make her browned buttered oysters.

She once gave an absurd description of her sense of shock when she discovered that she was grown up, or at least was growing no more, and that she was not "tall and graceful" nor did she have curly hair, as all her aunts had. She had assumed of course that she would be like them and hated the prospect of plodding on without this charming equipment.

After she completed the Rockford High School, Julia attended Rockford Seminary as a day pupil for one year, but she wanted to go to Vassar which was the first of the women's colleges and much talked of in that decade so given over to the discussion of the education of women. Her father was rather pleased by Julia's independence and was quite willing to have her go where she wanted.

Although in addition to the year at Rockford Seminary, she had a German tutor who came to the house every day and also Robert Rew, later Mayor of Rockford, who taught her mathematics, Julia later realized that she was not properly prepared for college. However, she entered the sophomore year at Vassar and through hard work graduated three years later, in 1880. Most of the members of her own class had entered from the Vassar preparatory school then conducted in the same buildings with the college, and had already formed a circle of their own so that Julia was inclined to be lonely. She found it rather difficult to address everyone with the prefix of Miss, for the girls at Vassar College were never called by their first names although Miss Smith and Miss

Jones might become the best of companions. Apparently this formality was part of the solemn business of higher education for women.

Her sister Anna went back with her for the last year at Vassar. The seniors roomed together in one corridor that entailed certain privileges, but Julia in order to live with her sister had taken two rooms with dormer windows located in the very roof and here she apparently obtained something of the freedom of her old home life. At that period students had more or less given up croquet and archery and the new game of lawn tennis had hardly arrived. They therefore took their exercise largely by walking an hour a day, usually two by two, and for this they made their arrangements long in advance. Some of them remember that Julia was very fond of walking with two Japanese girls. She had several warm friends among the faculty and always spoke of Dr. Maria Mitchell with the greatest admiration. There is no doubt that a real intimacy obtained between them.

A fellow alumna, Mrs. Andrew MacLeish, who was a senior the year Julia Lathrop entered college, writes:

> I have been able to find very little of Julia Lathrop's days at college beyond the fact that her friends were made largely outside of her own class. After her graduation when she went back on various occasions she was universally regarded as a distinguished alumna and there are many stories about her. It was Julia Lathrop certainly who sowed the seed which has resulted in the large and important School of Euthenics which is held at Vassar every summer to which mothers and a few fathers and teachers come every year bringing the children who are cared for in a nursery school. It is really a very important and fruitful work.

Mrs. Stanwood, one of her own class, writes of one such occasion:

> I was attending a reunion at college and chanced to meet Julia Lathrop in the hall of the first floor of Main. It came out in our conversation that she was about to address a meeting of the Alumnae Association in Assembly Hall but in her modest way she protested against my going to hear her speak saying that she had no idea that people would be interested in her subject and questioned how it would be received. Later, seeing her again and asking her about the meeting, she explained that she did not know how it had affected

most of her audience but that one woman, a trustee, had sent her word that what she had said had fallen in exactly with ideas of her own and had invited her to dinner that evening at Alumnae House in order that they might discuss the matter together. The next day Julia told me that she was supremely happy, for the outcome of her speech and her meeting with Mrs. Blodgett afterwards was that Mrs. Blodgett had agreed to back her idea with money and influence and was preparing to give to Vassar the building and equipment which were necessary in order that the students might have thorough instruction in the care and nurture of children.

The following excerpts from Julia Lathrop's speech on this occasion will I hope carry something of the plan and scope of the new department:

> Are some of you thinking that, after all, wisdom makes its own contribution through the individual to the home finally; that good parents—the only numerous class of parents—create good households; and that the natural devotion of mothers can still be trusted?
>
> May I reply that mother love can be trusted but that we presume upon it. Maternal affection is the most precious survival of instinctive life. By its motive power millions of women daily perform miracles of patient toil but Nature has withdrawn from the human mother the instinctive wisdom which, as Fabre has shown, she bestows so lavishly upon the hymenoptera.
>
> What may we not hope for the culture of the race when we put at the service of the human mother's intelligence the continually growing discoveries of research?
>
> I do not propose a small thing nor a cheap thing in urging that the present status of the education of women demands a new specialization to be signalized by the creation of centers of study and research in the service of family life. It means not only great endowment of money, it means the greater endowment of trained minds set to the task of working out the expedients of fashioning the tools of expression by which that profound maternal instinct, reinforced by intelligence, may freely work out the destiny of the young of the race.
>
> It is no less than a revolution which is implied. Its aim is to give the work of the woman head of a household the status of a profession. The change in this direction has already begun and I have referred to the many beginnings of teaching applied household eco-

nomics as a sign of the coming change. The question is whether the women of the higher education shall strengthen the movement directly and avowedly.

Earlier, when individual development was the goal of education, how often was it said of a woman, "Now she is married. What good will all that education do her?"

With the highest education creating great centers of study through which to utilize and coordinate the observations of mothers, do we not begin to see at once a new application for the higher education?

Mothers of the next generation will need not to resign themselves to the limitations of their fate but rather to equip themselves for its illimitable opportunities. Instead of being isolated by the narrow life of home, through it the mother allies herself to the highest studies and makes invaluable contributions as a sheer by-product of her daily cares.

The legal emancipation of woman is coming fast. The rapidity of her further educational emancipation rests with herself. Now it is partial; the recognized professions she may enter—those which will always invite a small minority of women. It is for her to make the great occupation of women a profession, to see that the highest education trains those who shall contribute toward that profession's success.

The initiative for the highest education applied to the service of the family rests with women. The carrying out must be done jointly by men and women since, diverse as may be their daily tasks, the interests of men and women cannot be separated; both are joined in the great onward march of the race toward that mysterious end which we love to call justice.

At the fiftieth anniversary of the College Julia Lathrop was given a prominent place on the platform. As was her custom at those times when "speaking was unduly prolonged" she took a refreshing nap but was suddenly awakened by the vigorous handclapping of the audience in which, in order to cover her confusion, she hastily and heartily joined. The audience, which was approving a statement that Julia Lathrop was Vassar's most distinguished alumna, at once "caught on" and added delighted laughter to the applause.

Vassar College has erected a beautiful tablet to her memory in Blodgett Hall with the following inscription:

TO

JULIA CLIFFORD LATHROP

a.b.   a.m.   ll.d.

class of 1880

nationally and

internationally known

for her distinguished

service in behalf of the

welfare of children

her alma mater

inscribes this tablet

It was very characteristic of her that the only reference I ever heard her make to this was to tell of her collapse when she saw that the tablet had given her a Ph.D. She said that she spent a sleepless night trying to determine whether it would be cheaper for her to go in for a Ph.D. at so late a day or to have the letters chiseled off the tablet and finally decided on the latter course as the quicker and surer. The A.M. on the tablet she had received at Yale University in June, 1918, at the same time that an honorary degree was conferred upon Madame Curie.

Two of her Vassar friends she saw much of after leaving college; one of them, Martha Hillard, succeeded Miss Sill as president of Rockford College and after her marriage to Mr. Andrew MacLeish, Phoebe Sutliffe, another of Julia Lathrop's Vassar friends, became its president. I insert here a vivid description of the Lathrop family life written by Mrs. MacLeish who was a frequent guest in the Lathrop home during her presidency of Rockford College, and another description contributed by an intimate friend of her brother William. We all know that family difficulties are easily developed when children are grown up and begin to find their individual interests often widely diverse from those in the family tradition. In a household composed of parents and adult children it is much more difficult to maintain a warm and understanding family affection than it is during an earlier period of family life. Mrs. MacLeish writes of the Lathrop home: "Julia's strong passion for righteousness and sympathy with suffering was developed in that home. She had her father's brilliant mind and he and she were most sympathetic. It was a lovely home life, quiet, restful, based on the real things of life which gave it solidity but lightened by a delightful sense of humor. One thing that impressed me was the respect which each member of the family had for the others and for their opinions. It was just the atmosphere for the development of a Julia Lathrop." The friend of her brother writes:

> I had the privilege of knowing Miss Lathrop in her home. The Lathrops were very kind to me and when I was a student at the University of Wisconsin I spent many vacations there. It was a home of the highest culture and the finest family life. Julia Lathrop lost none of her womanliness by being a public servant. The relationship and the comradeship between her and her sister and her brothers was ideal. Her devotion to her parents and their pride in her and regard for her was a beautiful thing. One discovered in the Lathrop home that Julia was widely cultivated; that she was a lover of art and believed in beauty but she believed at the same time that the most beautiful thing in the world was a race ennobled.

During later years when Julia Lathrop came and went from Hull-House to her pleasant Rockford home, her father once met one of her fellow workers at the Rockford railway station. As they drove along he said in his lawyerlike, quizzical way, "You don't seem to have anything the matter with you!" And then he went on, more whimsically, "Oh, well, when Julia asked me to stop at the station for you I looked for someone who was lame or blind or insane or something like that! You know we think she's only interested in people who are in trouble!"

After graduating from Vassar College Julia Lathrop went into her father's office to act as secretary. As he did not like writing and as this was before the days of stenographers, Julia did much writing for him. Later however as the office was equipped with modern facilities Julia read law, and the office itself admitted that "she knew a good deal about it," which was high praise especially from her brother Edward who was already established there as a law partner after careful professional preparation. Julia was in her father's office for several years during which time she was secretary for two different companies founded upon inventions by Rockford men. She had some stock in both companies and made money out of them both for the stockholders and for herself, because she was always shrewd and careful in business and enjoyed the sense of independence which her own income gave her. The career of teaching which attracted so many of the early college women never appealed to her although at one crisis she undertook some administrative work for Rockford College and of course did it well.

The family spent their summers in Rockford. Like most men of his generation Mr. Lathrop did not understand the need for a definitely arranged playtime. "Books and reading" were his own greatest recreation. There was always, however, driving, skating or dancing, although the last was not much in Julia's line.

There is no record of her inner readjustments during the eighties, those first years after college so difficult for many gifted young people, of which the Illinois prairies afford a touching example in the early letters of John Hay written from Springfield after his return from an eastern university. These letters which have been published under the title "Poet in Exile," are most illuminating as to the sense of isolation so often experienced by the children of pioneers after their first prolonged contact with an older type of society.

Whatever Julia Lathrop personally experienced she never told, and I had only my suspicions when I heard her talking so understandingly to young people who insisted upon self-fulfilment and upon the "luxury of personal preference." I also made a shrewd guess when I once heard her express the hope to a progressive educator that the colleges might at last cease to dig that ancient chasm which yawns so wide between the preparation for life and actual life itself. She added almost confidentially that consciousness of this assumed difference often handicaps the ardent youth just when he most needs the use of all his powers to make his adjustment.

I never heard her refer to any brooding sense of isolation although all self-centered musings might well have been put out of her mind forevermore in 1886 by the startling reaction to the Haymarket Riot in Chicago which introduced dynamite into the social conflict and so terrified the entire region that it exhibited symptoms of shell shock for decades afterwards.

It is of course difficult to estimate the effect of the Haymarket Riot

upon a mind like Julia Lathrop's which must have been already preoc-
cupied with the eternal question aroused by the inequalities of human
existence. I was myself an invalid during much of the decade of the
eighties and was abroad during the year of the Riot and the hectic year
following, but the Haymarket Riot belongs in this early chapter because
of its profound influence upon the social outlook of thousands of people, an influence which she shared.

The widespread fear and mass hysteria following the execution of
four anarchists and the imprisonment of four others remained an important factor in a social struggle extending over decades and served
for many people as a justification for wholesale hatred against foreign
radicals because they were all considered anarchists. It became a patriotic matter to denounce the eight-hour day, higher wages and col-
lective bargaining as anarchistic plots to destroy American institutions.
This hideous disaster also greatly accentuated the conventional hostility between the huge city and its neighbors, affording such dramatic
proof of the wickedness of Chicago that the down-state legislators for
many years not only deliberately prevented the city from obtaining the
legislation which it so often needed but denied it the freedom to leg-
islate for itself.

In the winter of 1888–89 when Ellen Gates Starr, an old friend from
Rockford College, and myself were advocating a new Toynbee Hall and
were asking our old friends for their co-operation and understanding,
we naturally spoke at Rockford College. As I recall that initial meeting, Mr. Lathrop although very friendly was not convinced of the usefulness of our plan but he assured us of his good will and made no ob-
jection when Julia decided to go to Hull-House.

4

Early Days at Hull-House, 1889

In beginning the recital of Julia Lathrop's life at Hull-House, I am not unmindful of the statement made recently by a biographer that he was "apt to drill his memories into a consistency which facts do not justify." This may easily be true of the writer of the following pages in regard to incidents, but throughout Julia Lathrop's entire life one estimate of her character never changed and I could dip in anywhere to illustrate her disinterested virtue. It is the phrase which comes most often to my mind to describe her unfailing sense of moral obligation and unforced sympathy. It is that sort of disinterested virtue which has been designated as "the refusal to nurse a private destiny," or in more recent phrasing as "a complete freedom from egocentric preoccupations." It was once described by a well known historian as the doctrine for which men have been persecuted and disgraced, the doctrine which tyrants condemned as rebellion and bigots as heresy, but there it remains to confound us all.

My earliest impressions of Hull-House include Julia Lathrop. Though she did not come to live in the settlement the first year, her sympathetic understanding of its purposes and her co-operating spirit in all its activities surrounded it from the beginning and became an integral part of it, from the very day of its opening in the autumn of 1889. At that date American cities had begun to exhibit the overwhelming and unprecedented problems of mass industry, which included overcrowded tenements, widespread misery in the periods of unemployment, the lowered health and vitality resulting from long hours and low wages and many other features so familiar to us now. This was due partly to the fact that during that decade 1880–90 the number of industrial employees in the United States had doubled that of the previous ten years.

In our efforts to enrich the lives of the tenement dwellers we organized cultural classes of many kinds at Hull-House and among the first educational groups was Julia Lathrop's Plato Club which met on Sunday afternoons at four o'clock, ending supposedly at six but sometimes continuing until ten. The reading was from Jowett's translation and the discussions ranged far and wide, almost confounding John Dewey himself, then a young professor in the new University of Chicago, who occasionally led the club. The membership was composed largely of elderly men who had read philosophy of sorts all their lives and had made up their minds regarding the purposes of the universe. One member who always disagreed with the class leader "on principle," as he proudly stated, was once betrayed into a speech which sounded as if he and Plato and Julia Lathrop were at last on common ground. When the latter expressed her pleasure to Mr. Dodge that he agreed with her he stuttered in his excitement, "I agree with you, Miss Lathrop, not at all, not at all— it is you who agree with me!" To lessen his discomfiture as the club evinced its amusement, she said gravely that it was of course important to know who had shifted his point of view—it might have been she or it might have been Mr. Dodge but she was quite sure that it was not Plato.

In 1893 we first heard the harrowing tales of refugees from the Kisheneff massacre and as the neighborhood south of Hull-House became ever fuller of Russian Jews fleeing for their lives Julia Lathrop's tender heart was wrung by their misery. Mrs. Hannah Loeb who represented a Chicago group of prosperous German co-religionists, established her first office at Hull-House where the piteous recitals went on for many days. Every effort was made to meet the emergency, sometimes by well-meaning neighbors with more zeal than wisdom. One of the few occasions on which I saw Julia Lathrop display real indignation was when a group of the forlornest refugees came with an interpreter to complain to Mrs. Loeb that it had been discovered that the soup given to them at a Canal Street soup house was made of loaves of bread boiled in hot water which had first been saturated with lard. I heard Julia Lathrop who cared for no ritual herself exclaim: "Of course you would rather starve!"

It was in the very early days of Hull-House that in the late afternoon a young woman rushed through the door quite breathlessly to tell us that a girl in their tenement house was having a baby all by herself; she was "hollering something fierce; my mother says it is disgracing the whole house she is!" Our informant went on to relate that none of the women would go in to help because the girl wasn't married and that anyway none of them would call the doctor because the girl had no money and "the one who called him was afraid that she would have to be the one who paid him." In response to our inquiry about the girl's mother we learned that "she had gone to work on the north-side where she washed for a lady every week but nobody knew the address." There seemed nothing for it but to go ourselves and Julia Lathrop and I set forth leaving a resident at the telephone calling up a friendly neighborhood doctor. We found the poor girl alone in her agony and by the time the doctor finally arrived, almost at the very moment that the girl's mother returned from her work, the patient was lying quietly in a clean bed and the baby, having been induced to cry lustily, was having his first bath. As we left, the little mother feebly expressed her first word of gratitude by telling us that she would name the baby after us; but poor little Julius John died four months later on the Northwest side whither his mother and grandmother had moved because it would be easier in a new community to drape his existence with decorous fiction. I vividly recall through the distance of forty-five years that as we walked back from the tenement house stirred as we were by the mystery of birth, and seeing the neighborhood at its most attractive moment when the fathers were coming back from work, the children playing near the doorstep to be ready for supper which the mother was cooking inside, I exclaimed: "This doing things that we don't know how to do is going too far. Why did we let ourselves be rushed into midwifery?" To which she replied: "If we have to begin to hew down to the line of our ignorance, for goodness' sake don't let us begin at the humanitarian end. To refuse to respond to a poor girl in the throes of childbirth would be a disgrace to us forevermore. If Hull-House does not have its roots in human kindness, it is no good at all."

It was during our first winter that one night at three A.M. the telephone rang and a request came that two of "the ladies" should go to a neighboring transportation company whose premises were ablaze and whose horses had been badly injured. An insurance company wished to know how seriously the horses were hurt before they permitted them to be killed; it would take a long time to send over one of their own men but the ladies who lived so near could go quickly and the insurance company would promise to take their report as final. Julia Lathrop in relating our adventure always said that "J.A. walked bravely into the stable full of groaning, screaming horses, but could not open her eyes after she got there"; that she herself, overcome by memories of Old Bill, could not walk in but had opened her eyes when she looked in. At any rate the poor horses were quickly shot and a friendly police officer escorted us home through the prophecy of dawn. It is curious that I have always remembered that sunrise, illuminating dingy streets, with more vividness than other sunrises I have seen from far-famed points of observation—in the Himalayas, over Mt. Everest, for instance.

Julia Lathrop and I went together in the summer of 1892 to represent the newly established Hull-House at "The School of Applied Ethics" in summer session at Plymouth, Mass. The first college settlement had been established at Rivington Street, New York, almost at the very moment Hull-House opened its doors. It always seemed to us that it gave genuine validity to settlements that they were inaugurated so independently of one another on so nearly the same lines. The college settlement association was represented by Vida D. Scudder, Helena Dudley, Emily Balch, Jean Fine—the first head resident, and others; Andover House which had been opened two years later, by its warden Robert A. Woods who had recently returned from a residence in Toynbee Hall. His "English Social Movements" published after his return from London was almost a handbook in the first settlements and made it quite clear to us that by 1890 we were well behind England in all types of social legislation designed to safeguard standards of living for working people as we were behind in organizations for popular adult education. English social movements were further represented at the Plymouth School by Bernard Bosanquet, a genuine philosopher to whom the Charity Organization people were eagerly listening. Professor Bosanquet was not only a fine scholar but a practitioner of his own theories with his wife in the relief of the London poor then first called "the submerged tenth." Franklin H. Giddings of Columbia represented the economics tending toward the emerging science of sociology, a term first used that very year in connection with the new University of Chicago. Father J. O. S. Huntington who had recently founded the Order of the Holy Cross, was also a vigorous member of the little faculty.

Even thus early in the decade of the nineties the young people's movements in America in the church, in labor organizations, in philanthropic efforts as diverse as the settlement and the Salvation Army were all characterized by a desire to get back to the people, to be identified with the common lot; each of them magnified the obligation inherent in human relationships as such. Father Huntington later became a frequent visitor at Hull-House, but as I recall his vigorous moral teaching it was at the Plymouth School that I heard for the first time his brilliant formulation that "the essence of immorality is to make an exception of oneself."

I was naturally very proud of my colleague, Julia Lathrop, who was so able in conference and in debate and whose quick wit did much to dilute the moral intensity which at moments threatened to engulf us. I felt within me an early squirming of the wretched demon of institutional pride and although I knew perfectly well that to cherish that demon was dangerous and destructive I still exulted secretly that whatever "the eastern settlements" might be, no one of them could ever exhibit a resident so brilliant as Julia Lathrop.

When the stimulating sessions were over we returned to Chicago by way of New York City and took the two papers I had read at the school with the stilted titles of "Subjective" and "Objective Values of Social Settlements" to the editor of *The Forum* to ask him to publish them. Julia Lathrop urged that the idea we were trying to embody at Hull-House should be put before the country while settlements were still young and before we had time to confuse the public with half-achievements and partial failures, probably in the end establishing merely that good which is the enemy of the best. She asserted this as we entered the building that housed *The Forum*. Never was a callow writer "peddling her own wares," as I scathingly said to myself, more embarrassed and weak-kneed and never was a friend more valiant than the one who conducted me. Even as we waited in the inner sanctum for the great man to appear she adjured me once more, "Don't cave in, J.A., this is our chance to give the public the pure milk of the word!"

After a delightful interview with the editor, Walter Hines Page, in which Julia Lathrop cogently expressed her reasons for desiring immediate publication, much to our astonishment Mr. Page took both articles and afterward sent a generous check in payment which astonished us even more. The articles were later published in a book with other lectures delivered at Plymouth. The book was called "Philanthropy and Social Progress" by the leaders of the Ethical Society who had convened the school, but among our more radical friends it was long referred to as "a fine Victorian example of rose water for the plague," and this in spite of the fact that Father Huntington who was at the moment an ardent single taxer, had derided charity as much as Professor Bosanquet had urged its more scientific administration.

Through all these strenuous efforts Julia Lathrop's wit never failed. I remember an early incident at Hull-House when an old friend of hers brought a parrot as a present to our then new day nursery. The friend who was a little *triste* in leaving the parrot, detailed his many virtues and ended with the boast that he knew not one single swear word. To her astonishment Julia Lathrop said: "That lack in his education will soon be rectified in our nursery"; and then as if in quick defense of the children she softly quoted the quatrain from George Herbert:

> Children pick up words
> As pigeons pease,
> And scatter them again
> As God may please.

After the donor's final departure which had been impeded by many references to her dear aunt to whom the parrot had belonged, and who we were given to understand would never have tolerated a single oath in any nursery of hers, Julia Lathrop said reflectively that it was stupid to impute virtue to a heathen bird whose ugly beak was obviously fashioned for the most outrageous oaths and to imply that the innocent lips of little children could be sullied by any words they could possibly utter.

The parrot lived a long and blameless life in our nursery. I am happy to say that he never learned to swear, perhaps because he failed to utilize his opportunities.

It was always taken for granted among the early residents of Hull-House that Julia Lathrop did not take a radical stand in the difficulties between "capital and labor" as we baldly called them in those days. Her attitude may have been due to her early life in a thriving manufacturing city or it may have grown out of her tempered wisdom.

Her friend Judge A. A. Bruce, a professor in the Northwestern University Law School, who knew her both in Rockford and at Hull-House, states her position in the early nineties as follows:

> Her great advantage lay in the fact that she could sympathize with the problems of the employer as well as those of the employee and the unemployed. In a difficult era of social adjustment she was able to interpret to the so-called upper classes the needs and the ideals and the aspirations of the poor and of the newly arrived immigrant and at the same time reveal to those who were less fortunate or perhaps less burdened with the responsibility of business management and of social organization, the real heart of these favored classes. She understood the one class because of her own family environment. She understood the other because the genuineness of her human sympathy made it possible for her to know them.
>
> Hull-House was founded three years after the Haymarket riot. It was a period of transition, an age in which on the one hand materialism and industrialism and ostentation were at their height and in which on the other hand there was a growing interest on the part of the universities and churches in social problems. It was an age in which capitalism and socialism were being constantly contrasted.

It was, however, still early in the nineties, in May 1894, that she gave an address at the Conference of Charities and Correction held at Nashville, Tenn. I quote from the official report:

> I have said that Hull-House is profoundly interested in the labor movement. No one can live among working people and fail to see the increasing power of organization among them. Several unions of women have been organized at the House and in several cases the House has been able to exert a conciliatory influence in strikes. The trades-union must be reckoned with as a fact, and can never

be scolded or fought out of existence. It is not necessary to deny the crudeness and selfishness of some of its manifestations. It is necessary to remember that these qualities are rather universal. The trades-union needs, what we all need, a high ardor for humanity, a living belief in the solidarity of human interests. I do not know what modifications of our present economic and industrial life are to grow out of the labor movement, but of this I feel certain, that if the movement fails to develop reasonably it is the fault not more of those who direct it than of those who stand aloof from it.

She was an early, and enthusiastic member of the Women's Trade Union League. Of course she was wise enough to see the mistakes of labor leaders and the advantage that was certain to be taken of them, but she always considered labor organizations essential to the development of a sound democracy.

From her very first years at Hull-House Julia Lathrop most brilliantly displayed her genius for friendship with the very young residents for she possessed an unusual understanding of promising young people with a great confidence in their prerogative to right the old wrongs of the world each in his own way. There was always a mutual understanding between them. In the first place, she distrusted the tendency of those who are already middle-aged or approaching old age to assume that the old may instruct the young. Her respect for youth was so genuine that she recognized and utilized the possibility that the young may profitably instruct the old. It is said that we can all like the young or envy them or fear them, but to learn from them is more difficult. The conceit of experience, the pride in having overcome difficulties, gets in the way, and "if we do learn from them we almost hope they haven't noticed it." To be individualized is what the young demand above all; each one wishes to be understood and appreciated as a separate human being unlike anyone else in the world, which in fact is true of each one of them. The words written of an Oxford don might fitly have been written of Julia Lathrop that "as he turned his head from guest to guest at one of his lunch parties, one felt that a new universe was seated in every chair." The young people very much admired her brilliant wit and also had a vague conception of her goodness which never permitted her to use her wit to the disadvantage of another person. A very clever young man who is not often confronted by anyone who can match quickly his abounding witticisms, once said: "Miss Lathrop is so phenomenally quick in the uptake and on the return that she must think of a lot of awful mean things to say, but she never once says one."

Then too the young liked her tentative attitude, the complete absence of an air of giving them instruction. What was once said of a great scholar, that his method became more tentative as his grasp on reality tightened, was true of her. It was because she was so thoroughly committed to the eternal verities that she did not grow dogmatic about them. Many of the men and women who were of the staff of volunteer residents at Hull-House during Julia Lathrop's many years of residence and semi-residence there gratefully bear testimony to her wonderful capacity for friendship. Young people always left her very much pleased with themselves, which according to a French proverb made them pleased with her; if the proverb held, their pleasure quickly turned into affectionate admiration. She was quite convinced that one thing the young disliked was a pretense of youth on the part of their elders and that the pretense itself spoiled the relationship. I remember her saying that many years before when she called herself young she had been astonished to find how quickly she had grown old and venerable to the oncoming generation without ever suspecting it. She had been much entertained by this incident. When it had been suggested that her brother's youngest child be called Juliana after her two aunts, Julia and Anna, the infant's elder brother and sister were perfectly aghast at giving such an old, old name to a little baby! They stoutly contended that they would love their little sister even if she were called "Garbage" but they did not think it was fair to name her after such very old people.

I once asked her advice in regard to a young woman who would not undertake the work she could do effectively because she had an ambition which habitually vaulted beyond her capacity. She exhibited that curious consciousness of a youth so surrounded by his unfulfilled ambitions that he feels himself absolutely a part of all he might have been. It is very trying however to his elders when he insists upon being judged by these vague standards and refuses to test his abilities by the drab world. The case I had in mind was almost pathological but Julia Lathrop who knew so well that personal fulfilment is best obtained through devotion to impersonal causes, gave as her advice, "Don't disturb her, J.A., the ambition will gradually be transmuted into a solace which she will need desperately for her old age."

Francis Hackett who lived for several years at Hull-House gives the following description of her, after stating that Hull-House not only recruited strong characters, it was excited about them:

> In the third month of my residence I was told, "Miss Lathrop is coming! Miss Lathrop is coming!" as if it were an occasion for public rejoicing. I had never heard of Miss Lathrop; the name was a fashionable one in Chicago and I thought this was much too fawning. I did not know Miss Julia Lathrop of Rockford, Illinois, who brought with her such force, such warmth, such an almost roguish sense of the tragi-comedy of American politics. You felt she enjoyed the game without losing sight for one moment of the big end she had in view. Her brown eyes, so sincere but with a sparkle lurking in them, her slow redolent voice, her flavor of Illinois, gave her a richness which was valued by colleagues who had less vitality. Yet that almost Italian salience was only one kind of strength.

One of the longtime residents at Hull-House, Mrs. Kenneth Rich, writes of this quality:

> My first picture of Miss Lathrop was at the Chicago School of Civics and Philanthropy. She led into a room full of new college graduates a handsome young gentleman from the Philippines, Manuel Quezon, well known as the leader for Philippine independence. That picture has remained a vivid one, because it characterized Miss Lathrop's eagerness to let youth speak for itself—and speak with her sympathetic support close at hand. She gave youth her friendship and faith. She gave to youth as to all others credit for the accomplishments she herself inspired.

Dr. Edith Abbott relates the following incident:

> I well remember one very early summer morning, almost dawn, when she called some sleeping residents of Hull-House to a front window in the hall. We looked out to see walking down Halsted Street a young Greek in the white kilted skirt of Hellas, pointed and tasseled slippers, and a tasseled cap, piping very musically on some long reedlike instrument. The lad was evidently on his way home

from a national festival of some kind. But Miss Lathrop had been so moved by the wistful figure of the homesick young Greek and the flutelike melody that floated through the still morning air that she said: "When I looked out of the window I gradually saw the Attic plains stretching out there where last night we saw only the sordidness of Halsted Street." She apologized for calling us but she said she knew we would be glad to share in the experience of the mirage or the vision or whatever it was that she had seen.

I once heard her at a St. Patrick's ball in Bowen Hall talking to the senior member of the firm of architects responsible for all the Hull-House buildings. She waved her hand to the beautiful interior and said, "You have done well by us here, but you started to build a dance hall which seems to have resulted in a fine church, and when you built the coffee house which was to be a substitute for the cheerful saloon, it turned into a crypt." The architect replied that the base architecture of the saloon had always annoyed him; perhaps it was a good thing to start a reform at the very bottom with a crypt. And as for dance halls, he had always understood that the element of restraint was essential to good dancing; possibly the fine lines as the ceiling sprang from the sustaining pilasters would keep the dancers to the proportions of good form which the residents of Hull-House apparently had been unable to do through moral suasion. She thanked him for giving the explanation, but added that she sensed a danger that the architecture of the hall might produce a restraint so efficacious that the dancing would result in prolonged sittings-out, as the coffee-house crypt might induce reflections so sombre as to inhibit indulgence in our proffered ginger-ale and grape juice.

One of the young people recalls with much amusement her absurd habit of going to sleep in the early evening. Of course she was wide awake later at the time most people went to bed, and carried on her reading or writing far into the night, but this habit was associated with many amusing stories. A Hull-House resident tells of the first residents' meeting which she ever attended in which a matter of great importance, or so it seemed to her, was being discussed. Just before the vote was taken the Chairman said, "Will somebody kindly wake up Julia Lathrop to see what she thinks on this subject; her opinion is always so valuable."

Of course her friends came to Hull-House from various parts of the world. I recall a visitor, Dr. Berta Lutz of Rio Janeiro, who stopped to see Julia Lathrop on her way from California to New York. Dr. Lutz' father was the head of the National Museum in Brazil and she was taking to him a present of three horned toads. The toads were left down stairs to spend the night, but unfortunately the lid of the box had been removed in the interest of more air and naturally they all escaped. In spite of a veritable army of small boys who hunted in co-operation with the residents up stairs and down it took hours to find them securely pressed against the wall back of one of the steam radiators. Julia Lathrop's attitude of responsibility for the horned toads amused us all. One of the small boys inquired, "Was it a relation of Miss Lathrop's who lost them toads?" and his pal replied, "Of course it was;—it's the way my ma feels when my pa gets drunk and insults the neighbors; we keep telling her that *she* didn't say them vile things but she feels just as mean as if she had said them herself; that's the way folks always feel about their relations."

5

A County Visitor,
1893

❧ It was during the winter of panic in 1893–4 that I first saw fully revealed Julia Lathrop's profound compassion for her helpless fellow men and her sense of responsibility for basic human needs which afforded so much of the driving power back of her splendid abilities. In our first impact with dire poverty, both among working people who suddenly found themselves without work and their savings exhausted, and among the poor, always on the edge of pauperism, who at last found themselves pushed into the black abyss, we learned during that dreadful winter following the Chicago World's Fair that when all else fails and private funds are exhausted the county is under legal obligation to care for the poor. Julia Lathrop long before spring became a volunteer visitor in the county agent's office and was assigned for duty to the ten blocks surrounding Hull-House. Day by day she climbed rickety stairs and visited damp basements, for tenement house regulations at that moment were practically non-existent.

Her first experience with the situation in that district and through the county institutions is best told in her own words. The following extracts are from her chapter on "The Cook County Charities" published in "Hull-House Maps and Papers" in 1895. The book, one of the Library of Economics and Politics edited by Richard T. Ely of the University of Wisconsin, is now out of print. The "maps" were made from material collected at Hull-House by Florence Kelley who was in charge for Chicago of the "slum investigation" made by the U.S. Bureau of Labor, the papers were written by various residents at Hull-House.

The most spectacular proof of the poverty entailed upon Chicago by the general business depression of 1893, and locally by the inevitable human *débris* left by the World's Fair, could be daily seen during all the severer months of the winter of 1893 and 1894. It was a solid, pressing crowd of hundreds of shabby men and shawled or hooded women, coming from all parts of a great city whose area is over one hundred and eighty-six square miles, standing hour after hour with market baskets high above their heads, held in check by policemen, polyglot but having the common language of their persistency, their weariness, their chill and hunger. This crowd stood daily, unsheltered from the weather, before 130 South Clinton Street. Now and again a woman was crushed—in one instance it is reported was killed—and the ambulance was called to take her away. Once a case of smallpox was discovered and a sign hung out and the office closed for a day or two, but this did not frighten away the crowd outside. It only served to give the clerks inside a little chance to get their work up. When once the applicant penetrates the office, he is in the great dingy waitingroom of the Cook County Agency from whence is dispensed outdoor relief. He furnishes his name and address and is called upon later by a paid visitor upon whose report the fuel and ration are allowed or refused. Or, if the application has been granted, the market basket discloses its *raison d'être,* and the allowance of food and one bar of hard soap is carried hence, the coal being sent later from the contractor.

It is hard to go to the infirmary, hard to get relief from the county, but it is esteemed hardest of all to be buried by the county. The abhorrence of a pauper burial cannot be better indicated than by the fact that of the 607 inmates who died at Dunning in 1893 the funerals of 251 were provided by friends. Indeed the one general effort at saving in this district is that sorry speculation in futures called burial-insurance. Of course there are numberless lapses on the policies which make the business profitable. The dread of pauper burial is two-fold. First, the lack of religious ceremony and secondly, the loss of a great social function far exceeding in magnificence a wedding or a christening. The necessary cost of sickness and death is vastly increased by absolutely unnecessary items on the undertaker's bill. It is the hope of this anticipated pageantry which makes the burial-insurance collector a constant figure, threading in and out among the tenements and collecting his weekly premiums. "And to think," exclaimed a mother in a spasm of baffled prudence and grief, "that this child I've lost was the only one that wasn't insured!"

There is a constant criticism of the county relief office from the recipient's point of view. He says the coal is delivered slowly and in scant measure, that favoritism is shown by visitors, that burials are tardy and cruel; and the facts justify him.

There is doubtless a certain satisfaction to the philanthropist and sociologist alike in having touched bottom, reached ultimate facts, and this in a sense we have done when we have reached the county institutions. These are the infirmary, the insane asylum, the hospital, the detention hospital, and the county agency.

She describes in detail the inmates in the huge county institutions, the hospital wards into which the doctors were not permitted to bring students for instruction but where the word of the newest and rawest medical graduate might reign supreme. She describes—"ward 3-b with beds crowded together, others laid upon the floor and filled with a melancholy company of feeble and bedridden men and idiot children. It must haunt the memory of whoever has seen it." But what distressed Julia Lathrop most about the Cook County Infirmary was the regulation which separated an old couple, sending the husband into the men's side, the wife into the women's side. It allowed them to see each other once a week with the heavy netting of a screen between them through which, if not too deaf to hear or too feeble to shout, they might communicate with each other for half an hour. When it became her duty as county visitor to send an old couple into the poorhouse she found the situation almost intolerable. This was of course before the days of old age pensions, and those responsible for "Charities and Corrections" were so afraid of "outdoor relief" that it was considered iniquitous to care for such couples in their own homes because county funds could more cheaply care for them in the poorhouse. Such a state of mind affords one more example of the danger of administering any human situation upon theory uncorrected by constant experience.

She reports one spot in these huge institutions as follows:

There is a chapel in which a kindly old Catholic priest and various Protestant clergymen officiate. The solemn little room is always open, and after the early winter supper old people clamber painfully upstairs to say their evening prayers before its altar. For one instant the visitor is hushed as he stands before the door watching the straggling little procession of human wastage entering the dim apartment, and feels a thrill of thankfulness that these poor evidences of defeat and failure cherish a belief in some divine accounting more individual and generous than that of the sociologist and statistician.

And yet the Cook County Infirmary itself had its moments of quiet humor and even of boisterous mirth, perhaps in response to "that puzzling thing about life, that cheerfulness will break in." One story about the Infirmary I remember in connection with Julia Lathrop's pleasure when she found in a down-state county poorhouse an old man with his shoes on lying on his bed. The manager who was showing her around said, "William, William, you will do it!" She was delighted because at that moment in the Cook County Infirmary none of the inmates, however feeble and worn out they might be, were allowed to lie down on their clean and tidy beds in the daytime, and she remarked how much better it was for William than to be the possessor of a fine bed which was not to be used except at stated hours. She recalled the story of an old man in the hospital ward of an infirmary who during his long weeks in bed constantly insisted upon sticking his feet "into the open air," as he said. This became a subject of prolonged warfare between him and the nurse in charge of the ward who considered it her duty to breakup the perverse habit. When at last he was dying in the little room of the infirmary reserved for those who had reached the end of the road, with all the members of his family gathered impressively around his bed, his old enemy the nurse with great solemnity softly opened the door. The dying man turned his eyes upon her, made one final desperate effort and defiantly stuck his feet out of bed "into the open air," confident that she could not reprove him when Death itself was majestically standing guard to protect him from all pettiness.

She encountered in the county institutions what she so often found afterwards in the state, the need for better civil service regulation. With her fine sense of fairness she says: "The remarkable thing with our present system of appointments is not that abuses occur but that more do not occur. It gives one after all a new confidence in human nature that the demands of helplessness and insanity develop in unpromising material such excellent qualities of patience and self-control as are sometimes shown." She ends the chapter however with this plea:

> Yet all these activities unfortunately are considered primarily only as furnishing certain "places" to be filled by political preferment. The comfort, the recovery, the lives of all these thousands of dependent people hang upon the knowledge, the kindliness, the honesty, the good faith of those hired to care for them. How were these people hired,—in the open labor market, for fitness, by examination? Not even an Altrurian would waste words on such a question. These places are scheduled with the salaries attached, and each Commissioner disposes of his share of the patronage. Commissioners are not responsible for this method; it is not unlawful and it is convenient for them. They act from the pressure of public opinion translatable into votes and modify their actions according to the strength of such pressure. How many persons in the city of Chicago whose incomes make them safe from the possibility of a personal interest in these places ever visit them or perhaps know where they are? More, how many of them realize that their visits, their intelligent interest are all that is necessary to make these institutions give really good service? There is no maladministration so strong that it can persist in the face of public knowledge and attention. The public now has and will have exactly such institutions as it demands, managed exactly as its discrimination requires. It is as tiresome as that Carthage must be destroyed but it is as true, that the charities of Cook County will never properly perform their duties until politics are divorced from them.

I find it very moving that almost forty years later after Julia Lathrop's long experience in administrative offices she made the following statement in a speech delivered in the very last year of her life:

> We are still indifferent to the quality of public service. A merit system of appointments is evaded whenever and wherever possible. Yet a merit system means only some effective method of securing competent honest public servants, such methods as any successful administration of private business must employ.
>
> Public business has vastly increased in scope since the first civil service laws were written in the United States fifty years or so ago.

The present juncture with the growing tendency to enact social legislation is crucial in its need of a new public conscience as to Public Administration.

Even in the very first years of Hull-House we began to discover that our activities were gradually extending from the settlement to a participation in city and national undertakings. We found that our neighborhood playground, the very first in Chicago, was not secure until it became part of a system covering the whole city; better housing was as dependent upon rapid transit as upon a good tenement house code for which we had worked against many obstacles through the City Homes Association. When we saw a certain depressed district a little to the north of Hull-House disappear as if by magic because the people could move west with a cheaper streetcar fare to carry them back to work, Julia Lathrop said dryly that we were like the dress reformers who for years had in vain advocated short skirts for women and then saw the bicycle come in and actually accomplish the change in one season!

A thousand times during that panic winter Julia Lathrop saw that much more was needed than the county was equipped to supply, and although she was a faithful county visitor, meticulously observing the hours and rules all the more carefully because she was a volunteer, she did other things as well. Realizing that the efforts must be city-wide and inclusive of many people she actually revived an interest in the Charity Organization Society which had experienced such hard sledding in Chicago, and started the movement all over again in a little office not many blocks from Hull-House. In describing the general district, Julia Lathrop wrote:

> There is an overwhelming proportion of foreigners and an average wage-rate so low as to render thrift, even if it existed, an ineffective insurance against emergencies . . . we are led at once to inquire what happens when the power of self-help is lost.
> This immediate district contains on its western side the least adaptable of the foreign populations and reaches over on the east to a territory where the destructive distilation of modern life leaves waste products to be cared for inevitably by some agency from the outside. The preponderance of unskilled labor necessarily means the weakness of trade unions and mutual benefit societies, in short,

the inability to organize and co-operate. When we inquire then what provision is made to meet sickness, accidents, non-employment, old age and that inevitable accident, death, we are asking what some outside agency performs. Here is a foreign population living in every sort of maladjustment-rural Italians in shambling wooden tenements, Russian Jews whose two main resources are tailoring and peddling quite incapable generally of applying themselves to severe manual labor or skilled trades and hopelessly unemployed in hard times; here are Germans and Irish largely of that type which is reduced by drink to a squalor it is otherwise far above. Here amongst all save the Italians flourishes the masculine expediency of temporary disappearance in the face of non-employment or domestic complexity or both; paradoxically enough the intermittent husband is a constant factor in the economic problem of many a household. In this region west of the river and stretching on into the seventh, eighth and eighteenth wards, there are many streets where foreign tongues are more spoken than English, thousands of people who having their own shops and churches and theaters and saloons may be said hardly to come in touch with the commonwealth of which some immigration company has made them an unconscious part until they are given over as the wards of its charity.

In the midst of this district a young man who came to live at Hull-House from an eastern city where the charity organization society had already been successfully established, opened an office with the backing of a group of trustees assembled by Julia Lathrop. It was a difficult performance and although long before spring the main office of the new undertaking had been moved down town with three branch offices of which the parent office was one, it was years before the more advanced method of administering charity was established in Chicago and developed into the present satisfactory United Charities. In the efforts to effect this reorganization I recall an incident which I hope will reveal Julia Lathrop's methods. At one particular meeting we had felt our plans for what we considered a better type of organization stopped as it were by the complacency of the upholders of the existing Relief and Aid Society which had been active ever since the administration of the Chicago Fire Fund in 1872. In a closing speech I had told the story of Boston whose charities were so thoroughly organized that if a three quarters orphan were discovered today, tomorrow Boston would found a society for the care of three-quarters orphans. I added that if a three-quarters orphan were discovered in Chicago today, that tomorrow the Relief and Aid Society would assert that they had taken excellent care of all the three-quarter orphans ever since the fire. Julia Lathrop gave me a queer look as I sat down beside her and later I begged her to tell me what was the matter with my poor little story. "Nothing was the matter with the story," she replied. "It was a fine story, and at least half the audience enjoyed it immensely, but I was afraid that you told it to relieve your own mind, you certainly did not expect it to convert the Relief and Aid people to our point of view." She looked at me with quizzical affection, and added, "Inner irritation is so hard to suppress that an audience can detect it even in a joke."

It was probably one of the same meetings at which the speakers were introduced by an eloquent chairman who presented us in such charming and flowery phrases as could only be applied to the most beneficent of ladies bountiful. He of course secured his applause, but afterwards Julia Lathrop dryly remarked: "It is not very complimentary to either of us, J.A., but I am afraid that it is a true word that we are the more highly praised in proportion as we are misunderstood."

It was in connection with the office of this early Charity Organization Society that an incident occurred which could not but deepen her keen sense of responsibility for the disturbed and aberrated mind. The young man who came as an expert from the East disappeared from Hull-House one evening when he had gone out to post a letter. For weeks and months every effort to find him on the part of the police, his family and his Chicago friends proved utterly unavailing. The newspapers were inclined to imply dishonesty in regard to the funds of the "new fangled charity" with which they had little sympathy, but as his accounts were found in perfect order the charge was completely dropped. His disappearance was due to one of those strange cases of loss of a sense of identity and he was not heard from for thirty-five-years when he wrote to his brother from a western state where he had been living under another name without knowing how he had acquired it. His mind apparently had turned back to his early training in a theological seminary and for most of the thirty-five years he had been a successful clergyman. Neither his wife nor his parishioners had ever suspected any other personality than the one they knew. The very next year he came to see me when I was spending a few weeks in the West. There was no doubt that he was the same man I had known so long ago although after much difficulty he had finally decided to keep to the second personality as the course which would be least disturbing to him and his community. He died soon afterwards tormented to the end by double identity. During the many weeks after his disappearance, however, when the desperate search was being made, Julia Lathrop as the chairman of his board of trustees felt a special sense of responsibility, and when we learned from his family of his having experienced loss of identity twice before for short periods, we were driven to the conclusion that such an amnesia had occurred again.

I venture to record the incident because of its effect on Julia Lathrop who only a few weeks later was appointed by the Governor a member of the Illinois Board of Charities, which had general supervision of the hospitals for the insane throughout the state.

I recall a long conversation I once had with her during a charming drive down the Rock River from Rockford to the little town of Grand Detour, a drive associated with such unwonted leisure that it must have been taken during a day off in one of the annual sessions of the Hull-House summer school held for ten years at Rockford College.

She drove a horse very well but the journey to Grand Detour necessarily occupied most of the day and we had plenty of time to discuss many things. We had visited a large stone mill built by my mother's father, Col. George Weber, in the nearby village of Como. It was still standing then although long abandoned as a mill. I told the story as I had once heard it, that after the huge mill was erected and the farmers brought their wheat from all directions the owner discovered that there was no market for the flour. The bran was more easily taken care of for it was often thrown into the Rock River and merrily floated its way to the Mississippi but the "haul" to deliver the flour either in Chicago or Galena, the two possibilities, was far too long and the railroads had not yet arrived. Col. Weber who had had a mill in the Lehigh Valley in Pennsylvania, where he was considered a successful business man, had apparently not been able to envisage the conditions in the state of Illinois in the 1840's. After all, why did pioneer Americans feel so superior to pioneer immigrants? Col. Weber's lack of understanding of the changed situation between Pennsylvania and Illinois was similar to the immigrants' ignorance of the differences between Naples and Chicago, between Bohemia and Iowa, and yet the immigrants living all about Hull-House knew little of the difficulties encountered by American pioneers although their own difficulties in a new country loomed so large.

We talked quite seriously of how we might some day write about the traditions of northern Illinois and the life of the pioneers there, so essentially like pioneer experiences in every part of the world, that we might demonstrate that an outdoor peasant from Italy or Poland might find it quite as hard to give up his self-directed activities for the mechanical work in a factory as an American boy found it to exchange his farm work for riveting a small wheel into a watch, as many of them were doing that summer in the two watch factories on the Rock River. The immigrants also cherished their peasant independence and grew restive under the conditions that made them interchangeable units in a great factory.

It may have been partly the result of this talk that at the next Old Settlers' meeting at Hull-House she gave a stirring address on the founding and development of Rockford as typical of early Illinois. One of her listeners was an old man who had spent his entire life as a sailor on the Great Lakes and could not get through twenty-four hours at a stretch without walking a full mile down to the lake shore in order "to look at the water." He was growing feeble and his wife, fearful that his waning strength would not hold out to bring him home each day, was very unhappy about the habit, and for years had never omitted her daily scolding on the subject. But that day as they sat side by side in the Old Settlers' meeting listening to Julia Lathrop, the exasperated wife had her first glimmering of his motive and he forgot his Americanism sufficiently to say, "I can understand how them foreigners might feel about giving up everything they had been used to all their lives, just as we do." Julia Lathrop had made human and understandable not only the pioneers but their successors as well. She was anxious that people should not forget the past but she did not want the past limited to their own narrow tradition of one class or nation.

In the same way the settlement believed that Americans could best understand the immigrants through free association and the discussion of common problems. We stuck to this at some cost, for such discussion often evoked strange preconceived opinions and untoward experiences.

6

The State Board of Charities, 1893

∂∂ In 1892 the Governor of Illinois appointed Julia Lathrop a member of the State Board of Charities and she assumed the position July 1st of the next year. She rendered distinguished service from 1893 to 1909 with an interim of four years, a service which was, in the words of Dr. Graham Taylor, "without compensation other than the heart's own reward for duty well done and opportunity well met." She visited every one of the 102 county farms or almshouses, discussing conditions with their superintendents and ameliorating for the inmates as best she might the evil effects which unjust suffering always produces. A friend once graphically wrote:

> One likes to think of her going the rounds of those dreary places, talking to the inmates and uncovering intolerable conditions which had always been taken for granted just because no one made it his business to do anything about them. One likes to think of the revelation she must have been to some of the stodgy officials who shuddered at the idea of any change. One wonders, for instance, what they thought of her when to test out a newfangled fire escape in an institution harboring helpless women and girls, she tucked her skirts around her ankles and slid down from an upper floor, to see if the thing really would work and not scare to death the fleeing inmates.

Another friend, Judge Bartelme, calls attention to "her quiet but really dramatic description of the conditions she found in the institutions for the feeble-minded and the insane; how she described the men and women, sitting against the high walls of the long corridors, rocking and rocking, all with their hands folded and staring into space because they had nothing else to do day after day." She gradually became an energetic leader in the movement to remove the insane from county institutions to the more responsible humane and intelligent care the state could give them in state hospitals, although she encountered incredible difficulties everywhere and especially in Cook County.

I recall her astonishment when among the state institutions she found a large orphanage for the children of war veterans. The fathers of the youngest of them had fought in the Civil War which had ended almost thirty years earlier but some of the veterans represented there were from the Mexican War and one of the older children proudly based his claim upon the War of 1812. The situation was explained of course by the fact that a pension-drawing veteran was considered a great "catch" and into his extreme old age, if eligible as a widower, was sure to be captured by an enterprising young woman who could be assured of a pension for "war widows and orphans" long after the death of the veteran himself. The large orphanage had developed gradually and perhaps inevitably but Julia Lathrop, concerned to secure the best possible care and education for these wards of the state, was often put to it in her efforts to give them something of the home life and individual attention that were afforded at the moment by the Illinois Children's Home and Aid Society of which she was a board member for many years. But like everything connected even remotely with war the orphanages were sacrosanct and to try to break them up for the sake of securing a more advanced type of care for the orphans themselves, was called unpatriotic, as was another effort which she made, that these healthy young mothers endowed with pensions for themselves and their children should be required to give maternal care to their offspring, as was afterwards successfully required in the terms of the Mothers' Pension law. Of course she understood perfectly well that she was being opposed by entrenched vested interests in the orphanages and she used to declare that there was no exaggeration in the story of the head of an orphan asylum who prayed that the Lord would send him many orphans in the next year so that he might erect a new wing.

Dr. Alice Hamilton tells of a visit in which she accompanied Julia Lathrop to an institution for the insane and her treatment of the inefficient management which she found there:

The experience has long served me as an example of the technique to be employed in visits of investigation. I used it for years
and still use it.

We were met by the Superintendent who was sulky and suspicious.
He did however conduct us all over his establishment and gradually
under the influence of Miss Lathrop's cordial and uncritical attitude
he thawed out; and presently he was pouring out all his troubles to
her, going out of his way to point out what was wrong and there was
plenty of it to point to. By the time we had returned to the office he
was in a softened and almost mellow mood and I, full of admiration
for her skilful handling of a difficult situation, expected her to de-
part leaving behind this friendly atmosphere. But I learned my les-
son then. Miss Lathrop sat down in the office and proceeded gently
but with devastating thoroughness to go over the whole situation
and point out to the superintendent that after all he was the one in
authority; if things were rotten it was he who must shoulder the responsibility, and she left him in no doubt at all as to how rotten she
thought things were. He listened with amazing meekness, having lost
all his truculence under her skilful treatment and being unable to re-
cover it in time. We left him evidently impressed and promising to
do his best, certainly not resentful in spite of her severity. Often since
then in my dealing with employers in the dangerous trades I have
felt myself tempted to rest content with the achievement of a pleasant relation in the place of an initial hostility, to look upon harmony
as an end in itself not simply a means to an end, then the memory
of Julia Lathrop's example has pulled me up and made me say the
disagreeable things which it is so much easier to leave unsaid.

In a little book entitled *Suggestions for Institution Visitors,* which was
published by the Public Charities Committee of the Illinois Federation
of Women's Clubs in 1905, Julia Lathrop drew on her own long years of
experience in her suggestion as to what to look for in visiting a county
poorhouse, a hospital for the insane or a children's institution.

Enella Benedict, one of the earliest residents of Hull-House, a teacher
in the Art Institute of Chicago, has been responsible throughout her years
at the settlement for a studio for eager young people, some of whom
have become well known artists and all of whom have found solace and
self-expression through a fine technique. Miss Benedict's interests however have been by no means confined to the studio. She says: "I remem-

ber how J. Lathrop used to sit like the angel at St. Matthew's ear while A. Hamilton wrote for the *Journal of the American Medical Association* about the insanitary conditions in public institutions and how J. Lathrop later, after the articles had been published, used to read clippings from 'a high American medical authority' at the Farmers' Institutes throughout the state."

There were several young physicians in the state hospitals for the insane who were well equipped professionally and eager to render the best possible service. They remember Julia Lathrop with much admiration and gratitude. Among them was Dr. Adolf Meyer in the hospital at Kankakee and for many years since head of the Henry Phipps Institute at the Johns Hopkins University Hospital. Dr. Meyer says of her:

> There are persons who do a tremendously important share of the world's work through what they are as personalities and characters. Through an ability to bring together elements who otherwise could hardly blend and do their individual share they create a meeting ground for achievement. Julia Lathrop was this type of personality, this type of character, and I was one of the beneficiaries of this rare gift through acquaintance and friendship ever since 1893.
>
> It was in that summer that Miss Lathrop became a member of the Illinois State Board of Charities and Correction, the first woman on that board, quite obviously appointed for merit because of her experience with Hull-House and in spite of the Republican tradition of her family. Her first visit to the institution was looked forward to with that curiosity which is apt to go out to a reformer. She proved to be an open-minded inquirer into existing conditions in the institution of 2200 patients and beyond that in the way the work was being carried on elsewhere; sparing of comment but congenial and with a happy humor never at the expense of others. The welfare of the patients and the efficiency of the nurses and the general administration and the work of the staff and the relation to the public were all equally represented in her attention. There never was a note of resentment or suspicion or fear of any impulsive recommendations; on the contrary a sense of absolute fairness and constructive helpfulness. When Weir Mitchell launched his famous 1894 address to the Association of Superintendents (now the American Psychiatric Association), Miss Lathrop helped me get a hearing for all the physicians—a discussion from the inside instead of the usual

counsel of perfection proffered from outsiders, probably the first time that the actual workers had been asked to offer their own ideas and vision.

Dr. Meyer has kindly sent a number of letters he received from her concerning many matters including the retention of the research laboratory which was constantly threatened by the politicians. Dr. Meyer says of these letters:

> The letters do not give much of an idea of the earnest and constructively minded rôle she played, because somehow Miss Lathrop preferred to discuss things orally rather than in writing. You can see from the letters how she took a very helpful interest in finding out all she could concerning any progressive activities abroad and here and in the personal needs in the work. She helped me to induce Governor Altgeld to have the staff members make a report of opportunities for improvements (published by the Department of Charities) and in many personal ways.

The letters reveal the discouragement she often experienced during her first years on the board. In one of them she writes: "There are a lot of such complicated things which I am feebly puttering over, unable to let them alone yet quite sure that the world is not really the better for my fussing and that I am rather worse. This does not sound very gay—and it isn't." Or again:

> I am really greatly bewildered by the political situation and quite at a loss how to steer my own small craft . . . I can't bear to broach the subject to my father. His disgust, not with me personally but with the situation, would be too trying to us both. . . . This muddle has started me down into a vale of discouragement where everything, including those high ideals of Americanism which we brandished before you, seems a part of the sawdust stuffing of the universal doll. . . . How is Keller? Have you read the ten volumes? Are the boilers in order? Tomorrow I shall fancy you in your laboratory. Here's to you and your snakes and doves. In that tower with your doves about you, you will be like the girl in "The Marble Faun." Have you read that story?

The following letter was written from a "down-state" county:

There is an awfully depressing and rather lonely side to this jour-
neying but if it were not for the poorhouses and jails it would be almost nice. This is an instance in which the charm of the play would
be enhanced by leaving out the character of Hamlet, for the weather
is delicious, the prairies are at their best and all the accessories are
fine. Yesterday I drove fourteen miles and back to a poorhouse. The
air was like wine, even the poorhouse seemed almost cheerful. I
quite longed for some companion a little less stolid than my driver,
but even he yielded to the crabapple's fragrance and said, "It did
smell awful good."

One letter is concerned with an individual case, a woman whom she
had tried to place in a home for incurables. She encloses a letter from
Mr. Higginbotham, the president of the board, regretting that they
could not take the patient. Julia Lathrop writes to Dr. Meyer:

Can't you go to see her and give your opinion as to whether the
mental condition approaches insanity or whether it is simply the
increasing feebleness of epilepsy quite without insanity? I wish you
were within talking distance this morning, there are many things
about the Detention Hospital matter which I would like to talk over
with you. I am very hopeful that all this may result not in mere quar-
reling over the trifling matter of two or three attendants' behavior
but in reality taking out of politics the care of the insane in the D.H.
The best practicable measure seems to me to be to get the commis-
sioners to turn the care over to the Illinois Training School for
Nurses. I know something better could be easily imagined but I
think this may be effected and I hope we can get some alienist in the
city appointed as visiting physician there. What do you think of that?

In another letter she writes:

I shouldn't inflict this uninvited attack if I had a little less assurance, I dare say, or if I wanted information a little less. Do you
remember once promising to tell me something of the sort of training given attendants in the foreign hospitals for insane? If you have
anything at hand bearing on that subject which would help an ig-
noramus floundering now and liable to be drowned in plain sight
of the County Board, I hope you will be humane enough to let me
have it. . . . Now here is something I have just thought of—it may
not seem as clever to you as it does to me: would you consider giv-

ing weekly lectures, or occasional lectures, before the nurses of the Detention Hospital?

In a letter concerning Dr. Meyer's offer of a position in Worcester which he finally took:

> If you were here I could give you a farewell dish of Institution gossip, very senseless in its causes but serious in its effects. It is not worth writing out. I shall try to see the Governor soon. I can't understand why so many disagreeable things leading to Nowhere seem to run to me as a way station. I am sorry enough to read what you say of Kkk [Kankakee] but it is like the rest I dare say. This necessity of earning a living sometimes holds men and women vice-like in such intolerable attitudes that one longs to embrace the program of any school of reformers which undertakes to minimize it.

Julia Lathrop was a brilliant *raconteuse* and her journeys through the state, especially that part sometimes called Egypt, afforded her fine material. She once asked the driver on a country wagon when she was riding through a southern county where she could find a telephone.

"We did have one between here and the next town but they never had anything we wanted and we didn't have anything they needed, so by and by some dumb scoundrel stole it for a clothes line and we never put it in again."

A man in the same county, with whom she was wading through almost impassable mud to visit the poorhouse, reproached her because she had not brought her high rubber boots with her, adding, "Every woman needs a pair, anyway, to do her milking in."

Such incidents entertained her hugely as did the remark of a boat captain on Ohio River, who said: "This morning you are in one town and tonight you will be in another town, forty miles away; how far do you expect to go in one day?" But she obtained more than entertainment; it gave her genuine courage when an old woman who, after a "visit outside" had persistently refused to go back to the poorhouse, returned at once when she heard that Julia Lathrop was expected to visit the county institution. She explained that she would have gone before if it had been known that Miss Lathrop was coming to "investigate" for of course she would give orders for more blankets; "She wasn't one to leave the poor to freeze."

She was concerned always about the care of the colored people in the public institutions. She used to say that while only a few of them would actually send relatives to these institutions, in imagination they all saw themselves or their children as possible inmates, and she added: "A state institution which discriminates unjustly against one colored man alienates from the state of Illinois the affections of hundreds of colored citizens." I have never known anyone who was so sensitive for the honor and evenhanded justice of public administration and who so persistently regarded inclusiveness as part of the ideal of public service.

In the years when she was visiting poorhouses throughout the state, trying to establish a farm for epileptic cases and more intelligent care for the insane, the residents of Hull-House recall that she wore what was almost a uniform, a dark blue tailored suit with Chinese blue shirtwaists, very becoming to her brunette skin, her dark hair and eyes, although we recall her once saying that in her next incarnation she intended to insist upon a blonde outfit because it seemed more useful in politics. She was always very well dressed by that ultimate test of good dressing, in clothes appropriate to the occasion on which they were worn. She believed that the public woman in her effort not to be careless had tended to become overdressed.

In addition to the hard work of discovering actual conditions and securing the much needed changes, she everywhere encountered the heartbreaking results of political corruption and the pull of self-seeking politicians. The state institutions were practically governed by appointed trustees who often lived in the town in which the given institution was situated. To be made a trustee had become a recognized method of rewarding local politicians who in turn took care of worthy henchmen by awarding contracts for coal, groceries and supplies and by appointments as gardeners, janitors and attendants to the inmates of the institution. "Of course these men cannot possibly follow through what all this means," Julia Lathrop once said,—"insufficient heating for people who are old and ill, poor food for growing children and, worst of all, neglect for the helplessly insane. If only because the attendants do not know how properly to care for their charges, they constantly yield to the temptation of roughness and cruelty." One man who as an institution trustee had successfully defied all her efforts to better conditions was afterwards elected Governor of the state. "His election only proves that using the state institutions for low-down politics is successful. From every other point of view his election is a dead loss," was her only comment. She always found Governor Altgeld deeply concerned for the unfortunate wards of the state and much interested in the better administration of the state institutions, although at the beginning of his term, when he had been besieged by the members of his political party "lean and ravenous from nearly forty years of enforced wandering in the wilderness," he had unhappily yielded to their demands. There was a widespread and quite justifiable indignation over the loss of Dr. Richard Dewey who had been for fourteen years Medical Superintendent of the hospital for the insane at Kankakee. My father had been a member of a committee sent from the Illinois Senate to locate a new institution and had insisted that the coming superintendent, who had been an assistant at the state hospital at Elgin, should be consulted in the construction of the hospital itself. Dr. Dewey had made it the first state institution in the United States to be built on a cottage or detached ward plan. During his administration he had abolished the use of restraint among the two thousand patients and had already made the beginning of a training school for nurses. All of this and other promising efforts in the state institutions were swept away by the change in political parties. Dr. Dewey's loss to the state was widely discussed not only because he was already a distinguished alienist but through an incident which only a few months before had brought the Kankakee hospital to the attention of the newspaper reading public. At Christmas, in 1891, the well known Chicago artist George P. Healy, had presented a number of portraits and landscapes to the hospital. This event was heralded throughout the country as it well might have been, and drew public attention to the fine work carried on at the hospital by Dr. Dewey, the knowledge of which before this had been largely confined to the medical profession and to experts in hospital administration. I have ventured to copy a paragraph from a fine letter in which Dr. Dewey expressed his appreciation of the gift to Mr. Healy: "You have conferred a distinction upon this hospital above all others of the kind in the world. To my knowledge there is only one that possesses any important work of a painter of the first rank. At Worcester, Mass., in the chapel there is a painting of Allston's also two or three good portraits of Miss Dorothy Dix and there is at Indianapolis a good copy of 'Pinel à la Salpetrière.'

That is all. Kankakee has therefore a great distinction." Governor Altgeld repaired the damage to the state institutions as best he could by energetically backing the first and only partially effective civil service law enacted in Illinois, which passed the Legislature in March, 1895. While this first Civil Service Law was only a permissive one to be adopted or not by the cities as they chose, a vigorous Civil Service Reform League in Chicago made it of genuine value after the city had adopted it by popular vote. It was however a decade later, in 1905, that its provisions were made applicable to appointees in state institutions.

Governor Altgeld attempted to accelerate this extension of the civil service provisions by a unique and somewhat naive action. In December, 1893, the Superintendent of every state institution in Illinois was directed by the Governor to make a thorough study of theories and methods adopted by the most advanced similar institutions in this country and abroad . . . to see wherein such institutions differed from ours and if anything was found elsewhere that was thought to be an improvement upon the methods pursued here, to at once adopt it; also to submit a full report of such investigation on or before April 1, 1894.

The resulting reports were published in collected form by the state and widely distributed so that it was believed that not only Illinois but the country at large benefited greatly by what was for its time and place a "unique experiment." This action was founded on Governor Altgeld's unwavering conviction that "wherever there is a wrong pointed out to all the world, you can trust the people to right it."

Affairs moved rapidly during those first few years of Julia Lathrop's office holding. A school for delinquent girls was established in Geneva, Illinois, in 1896 and with the constant participation of the State Board of Charities, the Altgeld administration broke away from the custom of increasing the size of hospitals for the insane and built two new ones, at Peoria and at Watertown. The Democratic Legislature also passed the first parole law in the state, the need for which Governor Altgeld in his experience as lawyer and judge had always felt very strongly.

In an address delivered twenty-five years ago, Julia Lathrop said:

> I know of no man in the public life of Illinois who did so much
> to give women an opportunity as John P. Altgeld . . . He did it be-
> cause he believed it to be right and he modestly never counted it

an achievement. One of Governor Altgeld's first official acts was to appoint women on state boards. He was the first Governor to name a woman as one of the trustees of the University of Illinois. He was the first to name a woman factory inspector. He insisted that there be a woman physician in every state institution where women and children were confined. All of these appointments had been swept away by the spoils system.

7

A Great Servant of the State,
1895–1909

🖎 In spite of the first attempt at civil service regulation in Illinois, it was the "spoils system" in one form or another, with which Julia Lathrop continued to struggle throughout her entire period of service on the Board. The situation may be illustrated by the experiences of Dr. Vaclav H. Podstata, who obtained one of the first professional appointments made in Cook County which were entirely free from political influence. He writes from California:

> It was largely Miss Lathrop who induced the State Board of Charities and the State Administration to arrange for competitive examination for the position of medical interne to serve in the various state hospitals. The first examination of that type took place in April, 1895. I had just graduated from medical college and had heard of this opportunity only a few days before the examination. The news interested me exceedingly but I entertained little hope of success. I doubted my ability to compete with those who had special preparation, but even more I feared political and other influences which I was told were always at work and would have much to do with the appointment. However, I appeared at the place and hour for the examination. The examiner happened to be Dr. Adolf Meyer. I presented my situation to him very frankly but with shaking knees. However, Dr. Meyer merely smiled and in his usual hearty way assured me that he had no objection to my taking the examination and couldn't see any reason why anyone else should object. He added that it was entirely up to me. This assurance naturally reduced my fear although I did not feel free from it until I received the no-

tice that I had been successful. I was certainly very lucky in receiving a position as interne at Kankakee. It brought me in personal contact with Dr. Meyer. There was no longer any question about this examination being without favor. I had not the least bit of political influence and was practically unknown to any prominent member of the medical profession.

We were not overly nicely received at Kankakee by the Superintendent, Dr. Gapen. He declared quite frankly that he had not asked for us and that he was quite able to make his own selections of medical assistants.

𝒟

Dr. Gapen was succeeded by Dr. William P. Stearns, who made an earnest effort to elevate the scientific work of the institution. However on the pretense of a minor disturbance in the institution, his political enemies succeeded in compelling his resignation. It was largely from that time on and up to 1902 that the conditions at the institution became unbearable. The food served the patients was often uneatable. During the summer, especially when some political campaign was going on, large numbers of our attendants were dressed up in duck trousers and blue serge coats, equipped with canes and set out to do special marching at county fairs. Attractive women attendants were trained to dance maypole dances. There were times when our attendant forces were reduced to unsafe proportions.

In the meantime politicians were building up tremendous political machines and incidentally were not forgetting themselves. Some remarkable things happened. On no salary, certain public officials became quite well to do if not actually rich. Also they succeeded in building beautiful residences for themselves and paying off their old debts. These conditions induced Miss Lathrop to start an investigation at one of the state hospitals. This occurred in 1902 after I had left the hospital. A perfectly tremendous effort was made to prevent the charges from being proved and everything was done to intimidate witnesses. I was requested by Miss Lathrop to appear as a witness. Almost at the same time I received a threatening message from the political circle of that institution. I was threatened with arrest and imprisonment on all sorts of charges if I dared appear. However, I did appear and testified. I received a letter from

Miss Lathrop thanking me for my appearance and testimony although I was prevented from testifying on certain important matters which should have been considered.

Shortly after that I received a telegram and a letter from Miss Lathrop urging me to reconsider my refusal of the position of superintendent at Dunning. My refusal was based upon the urgent advice of some of my friends not to accept a position so notoriously political and impossible. I was told that everyone else had failed and I would undoubtedly be broken also. Another reason was an attractive offer in terms of salary and better position at the Lake Geneva Sanatorium. However I felt that with Miss Lathrop's support I should have a fair opportunity at Dunning and therefore I accepted, occupying the position on July 1st, 1903.

Of this appointment Dr. Hugh T. Patrick, a leading alienist in Chicago, said at the time: "A medical man without pull, on the mere recommendation of medical men equally without pull, has been appointed to a most important position in the county." Of course it could not possibly have taken place without the staunch co-operation of the physicians of Chicago and of the newly elected "reform" county board of which Henry G. Foreman was President. A very touching letter was written to Dr. Podstata by Julia Lathrop before his decision was made. After congratulating him upon his recent marriage with the concluding phrase, "I hope that I may meet your wife soon, and while I congratulate you upon general principles, I would like a chance to congratulate her personally on the basis of all the good things I know about you—" she writes further:

> I am very sorry to hear tonight that you feel that you cannot afford to leave Lake Geneva. Is your decision final? The other place needs the right man so tremendously and the crisis is so great that I confess that I had just allowed myself to believe that you would take it. I am back in town tonight from a week in Rockford and Dr. Billings has called me up by telephone to say that you feel you can't come. There is much to repel about the place of course, but not the sort of thing to repel you. However I know that you have considered carefully and I am not venturing to urge a different decision.

I am sorry that you can't come and trust that you and Mrs. Podstata will come to Hull-House some day when you are in town.

Like other early laws for the better regulation of civil service the first provisions for Cook County often failed of their purposes and sometimes landed the adherents of the reform in ridiculous situations which were eagerly seized upon by the press. Thus Dr. Podstata on his first Thanksgiving Day as Superintendent of Dunning, objected to the mince pies produced by the baker in the infirmary, which led to a charge of inefficiency before the Civil Service Board. The newspaper headline, "How to Cook a Mince Pie, a Civil Service Problem" at least made the words familiar to a careless public, Julia Lathrop said.

In the summer of 1898 Julia Lathrop went to Scotland to see what she could of the Scotch care of the insane and especially their "boarded out" system. She also went to Belgium where she visited Gheel, a colony which had been known and described in medical and lay journals for many years but it had always been said that the village was necessarily unique and that such care could only be the result of centuries of experience fortified by an ancient and semi-religious origin. Julia Lathrop was therefore delighted with the new village colony Lierneux where a successful colony for the insane had been opened in southern Belgium to correspond with the one at Gheel in the north.

When we were abroad together in 1900 she visited the new colony in France at Dun-sur-Auron and another in the adjacent village of Ainay; she also visited colonies in Germany, especially the ones in the villages near Berlin and attended in Paris the conference on L' Assistance Familiale Urbaine pour les Aliénés Inoffensifs, held during the Exposition.

Two years later in 1902 she gave a paper on village care of the insane which is to be found in the annual proceedings of the National Council for Social Work.

The paper is most touching in its understanding of the patients themselves. She described her visit at Dun:

> At Dun on January 1, 1900, there were 654 patients, of whom four were men, but all the others were old women, for which class the colony was designed. I saw the village in June, 1900, eight years after

the first patients were sent. An old inn opened off the main street whose row of dwellings was broken on the opposite side by the church and a pretty, open square. This inn had been turned into a superintendent's house and a little hospital. In the big gardens beyond, another hospital for the care of patients who should become too feeble or too demented for family care was nearly completed. One assistant physician was with the superintendent; the other was stationed at one of the outlying hamlets where patients were boarded and from which he could more easily supervise his district. As we walked down the village street toward dusk, we met a woman leading a little child who hopped contentedly along by her side. The woman was a boarded-out patient and she explained that a neighbor was ill and she was helping her by caring for the neighbor's child. Notice that the patient was not the compelled nurse of her own hostess' child, but that she was lending her friendly aid to a sick friend.

The Superintendent of Ainay told her:

Some of our boarders work with their guardians in the fields, tend the sheep, the ducks, turkeys, etc., receiving in return gratuities— coffee, a few sous. But when work with the guardians is lacking, or if the patients do not want to work for them, they seek an occupation among the people of the village. We have those who cut wood, mow, work in the gardens, carry water, occupy themselves with household tasks. Some work with the shoemakers, tinkers, etc. An upholsterer has re-covered the furniture in all the salons of Ainay. One gives lessons in writing. We have one who keeps accounts and writes up the books of the town merchants. A former professor gives lessons in French to the children of two notable merchants of the place. An old regimental sub-director of music gives violin lessons. A mechanic repairs all the sewing machines.

She tells of a Scotch village:

In one of the cottages a vigorous old woman was seen. She was lighting her pipe at the fireplace with a comfortable air of possession. We were told that when first sent from the asylum she had been rather "wild," lifted her stick when crossed or annoyed, etc. Now she was a quiet, orderly person, much interested in some young lads who were also boarded in the house, and with her corner by the fire, her pipe, and her grandmotherly fussing over the boys she really had a nibble at some of the joys which appertain to old age.

In another cottage three men were boarded. The head of the house raised fruit for market, and one of the boarders who had been a gardener now helped in the kind of work he knew how to do. The men all came in to see the commissioner and the secretary, but one, John, soon slipped out quietly. The hostess said "Would you like to see where John is gone?" and took me through a passage and back garden into the neat cottage where her daughter-in-law lived. John was found sitting on a little cricket rocking a low wooden cradle in which slept a baby. The young mother said that the baby was fretful and she did not know however she could get through her work without John to "mind" him. That baby was John's supreme interest and patient care.

Not long after, I was visiting an American asylum of the usual baronial castle type, and in a locked ward of rather violent patients was an elderly woman of neat appearance, knitting very skilfully. I asked her where she learned to knit and she said with a jerk of her thumb, "About forty mile over there." When I confessed that I could not knit, she said, "Well, where was you raised?" and when I answered "At the northern end of the state," she retorted with a jovial smile to take out the sting, "Well do they work or do they steal for a living up there?" The attendants said she could live perfectly well outside "If she only had someone to look after her a bit."

In the main building a few hundred feet distant apparently, but really as remote as Europe, she had heard that there was a new baby in the family of one of the staff physicians, and she sent a pair of pretty socks of her knitting to this child she probably would never see. She was far more expensively housed than John. The great building in which she lived was set in the midst of a splendid park instead of a humble cottager's garden, her food and clothing came out of a far higher per capita than his; but as for me or my kin, I would choose the lot of John.

Julia Lathrop also drew the attention of the Conference of Charities and Correction to what she called unrecognized ways of placing out:

> In unrecognized ways there has been a placing out going on in our country for many years. For example, in visiting one of the Wis-

consin county asylums, I asked the superintendent if he thought boarding out was practicable. He said "No, I don't believe that would answer." Looking over the big farm where insane men could be seen working independently at half a dozen occupations, I said "Don't you ever send any of these men out to work for any of the farmers around?" "Oh yes," he said, "I've sent out about fifty in the years I've been here, and most of them have done well."

Perhaps it is only fair to the structure of this paper, so shot with personal understanding and sympathy, to quote from the conclusion:

> It will be noted that four distinct types have been mentioned:
>
> *First,* the Berlin system, in which an urban asylum boards out a fraction of its patients in close proximity—as in the suburbs of Berlin—retaining them under the supervision of its physician. This is valued not only for the lessening of cost and the relief to an over-crowded institution, but also because it affords an easy way-station for convalescents in the transition from the closed asylums back to the world. It is evident from the Memoirs of Dr. Marie that he hopes that some use of this method will be made by the hospitals of the Department of the Seine.
>
> *Second,* the Belgian villages, which receive both acute and chronic cases, without previous commitment to an asylum, and at Gheel at least, epileptics and imbeciles also, of both sexes and of varying ages. Both private patients and those dependent on the public are taken and accommodated according to former habit of life so far as possible.
>
> *Third,* the French village, Dun-sur-Auron, which receives only old women, and Ainay, its neighbor, which was opened in 1900 for men. Both men and women are those transferred from the closed asylums only.
>
> *Fourth,* the Scotch plan, in which from the Lowlands to the Hebrides insane persons transferred from the closed asylums are boarded in villages, in scattered farm holdings, with crofters, etc. Both men and women are thus cared for. The patients' care is paid for by the parishes to which they belong, and they are under the immediate supervision of the parish authorities, above whom is the General Board of Lunacy Commissioners with a force of physicians as visiting deputies. No locality is allowed to become known distinctively as one where insane patients are boarded.

It is important to note that in the four instances referred to there is a well-organized system of public care and supervision, and that the officers entrusted with the management of the system are not political appointees in the unhappy sense, but are civil servants who have undertaken a dignified occupation with its own responsibilities and rewards, absolutely removed from the domain of politics. Such a system and such a personnel are essential to such an enlargement of method in the care of the insane as is meant by boarding out.

It was when "spoils" politics had so interfered with the better care for the wards of the state she had so painstakingly established, that in 1901 Julia Lathrop resigned from the State Board of Charities as a protest against what she could not prevent. We were all startled by her resignation. I remember expressing to her my admiration, "J. Lathrop I didn't think you could do it," to which she replied, with a suspicious terseness, "I am not sure that I can." I knew perfectly well that she could not voluntarily have left all those helpless people, if her desire to secure them protection from political corruption had been founded upon the mere theory of civil service reform, but, based as it was upon a determination to save living human flesh from destruction, she was able to carry it through.

She resigned when Richard Yates became Governor of Illinois and Dr. Emil Hirsch, leading member of the State Board of Charities, resigned with her. To quote a leading newspaper of Chicago: "Miss Lathrop stood out always as a vigorous independent member of the State Board of Charities, and the newspapers in 1901 carried the news of her resignation when she thought the public welfare services were being prostituted for political purposes."

She had always avoided that pitfall for the feet of the righteous, the belief that she was indispensable to a given undertaking and that no one could take her place, although she, of all the people in the state of Illinois, might at that particular moment have been tempted to this devastating belief.

Her letter to Governor Yates in resigning her membership on the State Board of Public Charities adequately explained the reasons for her withdrawal. The letter which bore date of July 18, 1901, follows:

My Dear Sir: I hereby tender my resignation as a member of the Board of Public Charities of Illinois, and I beg leave to state at some length the reason for my action.

Since my first appointment on this board, rather more than eight years ago, there have been two administrations in this state, one of each political party. During all that period the institutions have been used for party ends, although the growth of political control has never been so apparent as now when there is another change of administration without a change of party.

The control of the expenditure of $2,500,000 yearly and of thousands of appointments would be a responsible task in any purely commercial undertaking; but when the money is to be spent and the people hired for the great function of humanely, wisely and economically caring for ten thousand sick and helpless human beings it is certainly worthy of skilled and disinterested attention. Yet it is common knowledge that the charitable institutions, whose cost is nearly one-third of the state's budget, are and have been for the last eight years "in politics."

When you expressed yourself publicly in Chicago before election as in favor of taking the charitable institutions out of politics many people were greatly encouraged; and when after election a friend of yours came to me, as he said, at your request, to ask what legislation on this subject the Board would suggest and stated that he knew you to be in favor of a merit system, I was again encouraged.

A bill was prepared by a committee of the Board which was urged by the press and which was recognized by its friends and foes alike in the legislature as being an honest effort to provide a workable rule for placing the institutions on a merit basis and for keeping the enormous contract expenditures out of politics. To the surprise of the committee, you showed no interest in the bill and, indeed, retarded its introduction until its passage or even its discussion was impossible. Your attitude in this matter was a keen disappointment.

I still trusted however that for some reasons of expediency you desired merely to postpone new legislation on this subject. The memorable example of the lamented Governor Mount of Indiana, who spoke in Illinois upon this subject last year at two important gatherings, showed that a Governor, by personal will and determination, could set the institutions too high for political arms to reach, and that without the aid of any law; and I again hoped that when the organization of our Board received your consideration you would then make plain to the public that you had begun a new policy.

It was however general gossip for months before the statement appeared in print that you had offered the secretaryship of the State Board of Charities to Mr. J. Mack Tanner. No name could have been suggested which would so intimately represent the standards and traditions of the preceding administration—into the details or the public disapproval of which it is unnecessary to enter here. His election yesterday by the barest majority—three members being present and two voting for him—was by your direction, as was stated in the meeting, and must be taken to be an explicit notice that no change of policy is purposed.

Board's Responsible Officer

I believe the new secretary to be an amiable and worthy young man personally but the Board must view its secretary as its responsible executive officer. He is the source of its information as to the accounts which it must approve and as to the general conduct and spirit of the institutions, and he holds the reputation of the Board in his hands. Why should the members of an unsalaried Board be asked to place their personal reputations in the keeping of an officer whom they have no voice in choosing? The law creating this Board is certainly explicit in its provisions that the Board shall independently select its employees.

When I came to the office yesterday I found a young man, grandson of the President of the Board, placed there by you as a clerk at a salary stipulated by you. I do not doubt that he is a worthy young man, but this clerkship is new to the Board, was created without its voice or knowledge, and the clerical work of the Board has been well done without it heretofore.

The Board is an unsalaried body of five persons, appointed for a period of five years each. This term was manifestly specified to preserve the permanency of the Board and its separation from Gubernatorial changes, yet the resignations of all the members, save of one whose term had expired, were requested by you in strict accord with the policy of your predecessor.

The Board has no significance unless it serves as a safeguard and guarantee to the public that the institutions are well managed and that the patients are receiving proper care. On the assumption of this guarantee friends of patients constantly appeal to me as a member of the Board. Upon the helpless patients and inmates comes the final weight of every unnecessary expense or extravagance, of every counterbalancing effort to economize unduly.

I do not resign because, as has been said in the press—perhaps truly enough—a dictated appointment is an insult to the Board. This is too important a matter for personal pique or even official dignity to enter, and I certainly have neither in this case. I feel however that my continued presence on this Board will appear at least to indicate a complacency towards methods whose evils I have seen too long and which I have tried earnestly, but of course vainly, to overcome. I am not willing longer to appear to the public, and far less to the anxious friends of patients, to give an assurance which no members of such a Board, however far they may exceed me in capacity, can give under the present system.

The work of the Board has become a matter of the warmest personal interest to me, and I leave it with pronounced regret and only under a conviction that it is my plain duty at this time to make such protest as I may against the continuance of a system which, from the Board of Charities to the last servant of the smallest institution, leaves no one free to do his task regardless of all save its faithful performance.

In point of fact the break was only temporary. When Charles Deneen became Governor of Illinois in 1905 she was restored to the Board and served five years more until the system of a salaried Board of Control was worked out in 1909. Several provisions of the charities act of 1909 were a great satisfaction to her. The Charities Commission was given general supervision over a board of three non-salaried visitors, one a woman, for each state charitable institution. The visitors were required by law to visit the institution of which they were visitors monthly if it served a district or part of the state and quarterly if the institution served the entire state. The State Commission was also given supervision over boards of county auxiliary visitors whose duty it was to visit annually and report on the jail and almshouse in their county.

She was also happy over the distinguished personnel of the Commission which was appointed by Governor Deneen early in 1910. It was composed of Dr. Frank Billings, Dr. John T. McAnally, Dr. Emil G. Hirsch, Mr. John B. Harris and Mr. John N. Rapp. Three of them had been members of the State Board of Charities from 1906 to 1909 and were well informed, as she knew, on the state charitable service.

It was years later, however, before the colony for epileptics for which she had worked so long was finally established. The act was passed in May, 1913, and went into effect July 1st of that same year. It repealed an act which had been passed April 19, 1899, from which so much had been hoped and which had been found to be unworkable, largely because of political ambitions for its location in various parts of the state.

That Julia Lathrop's position in the end was understood is made clear in this editorial from the *Chicago Daily News:* "In all her official positions Miss Lathrop insisted upon keeping patronage dispensers at arm's length. She was fearless and uncompromising in her independence, but she had tact and rare diplomatic skill. Her methods were adroitly conciliatory. She was a stanch advocate of merit in places of public employment and her humanitarianism was thoroughly practical." Mr. L. A. Bowen, Superintendent of Charities, State Department of Public Welfare, said of her in 1932:

> Miss Lathrop always has been an inspiration. Long before I ever entered the state service I knew her ideals and possessed considerable information on her methods in the state hospitals. I was a newspaper man here in Springfield during the Yates and Deneen administrations. The controversies that raged during those years over the administration of the State charitable institutions always were among my reportorial assignments. In that way I learned very much about these institutions and became interested in them. Finally when I became associated with them I was always more or less conscious that many of the things I tried to do had been tried out by Miss Lathrop. The fact is that even to this day our program in the State hospital consists very largely of the principles and the ideals which Miss Lathrop championed as early as 1900.

8

Friendship with Florence Kelley—
National Conference of Social Work

As the educational activities at Hull-House were gradually developed, we found many young people to whom it was useless to offer educational advantages because the promise of youth had been frustrated by premature labor or by malnutrition in childhood. It was not only the greed of employers but of consumers and even of parents which had to be curbed before leisure for education could be secured for such children, and it was perhaps inevitable that efforts to secure a child labor law should have been our first venture into the field of state legislation.

Florence Kelley who came into residence at Hull-House in the winter of 1891, galvanized us all into more intelligent interest in the industrial conditions all about us. She was especially concerned for the abolition of child labor and the sweating system and she urged such remedial measures as shorter hours, and the elimination of night work. Writing of her Edith Abbott says: "The method of social progress in which Florence Kelley believed almost devoutly was that of direct assault. She brought magnificent weapons to bear on the enemy. Sleepless, tireless, indefatigable, she was always on the alert. Life was never dull and the world was never indifferent where she lived and moved."

We all felt the stimulus of her magnetic personality and during that first winter the foundation of a lifelong friendship was laid between her and Julia Lathrop.

It was as a result of Mrs. Kelley's energy that a Commission was sent up from the Illinois legislature to investigate sweat shops in Chicago, and through the co-operation of the labor unions and other public bodies the first factory act of Illinois went into operation July 1, 1893, with Florence Kelley as chief factory inspector. Her deputy inspector Mrs. Stevens also lived at Hull-House as well as the attorney Andrew Alexander Bruce, who conducted the court cases on behalf of the state, and another stirring inspector, Mary Kenney, lived next door at the Jane Club; so we did not lack material to keep alive our interest in industrial conditions.

It was during the same winter after the World's Fair of 1893 that William Stead often visited us at Hull-House, and his brilliant monologues on a Sunday evening or at a prolonged dinner table were very exhilarating although his indictments offer seemed unduly severe. He had recently published "The Bitter Cry of Outcast London" and had been most unfairly sent to prison because of his methods of securing information. But he made us all very uncomfortable by his assertion that an international white slave traffic actually existed and had ramifications in Chicago. Some years later the fact was established with the finding in the Immigration Commission's report in 1911.

Mr. Stead was much struck by the way Hull-House seemed to have become the center of a fight against the smallpox epidemic which the World's Fair had bequeathed to Chicago. I quote from a description of this experience written years afterwards by Judge Bruce:

> I knew Florence Kelley at the time of the smallpox epidemic when both she and Julia Lathrop were risking their lives in the sweatshop districts of Chicago and were fearlessly entering the rooms and tenements of the west side and not merely alleviating the sufferings of the sick but preventing the sending abroad of the disease-infected garments to further contaminate the community. I saw these two women do that which the health department of the great city of Chicago could not do. The authorities were afraid not only of personal contagion but of damage suits if they destroyed the infected garments. They therefore said that there was no smallpox in Chicago. Later as the result of a joint attack by Miss Julia Lathrop and Mrs. Florence Kelley they were induced to act and they destroyed thousands of dollars worth of clothing. That attack illustrates the difference between these two tremendously useful women. Julia Lathrop, the diplomat, reasoned and cajoled. Mrs. Kelley, the fighter, asked me to file a mandamus suit to compel action. Each acted in her own way, but each fought for the same cause and each risked her life in the same conflict. Working together, they saved hundreds perhaps thousands of human lives.

One day I heard a young doctor remonstrate with Julia Lathrop that while she might consider it her duty to put the smallpox patients into the contagious disease hospital, it was really not necessary to follow them there and to be "a messenger of cheer between them and their families." She replied that there must be some human method of communication and that she certainly knew better how to keep free from contagion than their families did and that she had many more opportunities for cleanliness.

One of the Hull-House residents says: "Hull-House I verily believe was the most interesting place in the world when Julia Lathrop and Mrs. Kelley were both there. There were always Mrs. Kelley's quick characterizations for the benefit of the group of residents gathered about her after she came back from her night. school. All were packed into the Octagon, where Miss Lathrop would start one of her meandering sentences which, after amusing people all the way, suddenly wound up with some unexpected twist."

The persons who knew both of these brilliant women at Hull-House tend to associate them together and vividly recall the long and scintillating discussions between them not only when both were residents but long afterwards when they often met there. Their most doughty debates centered around court decisions. Florence Kelley constantly saw what she considered beneficent legislation thrown out by the decision of the supreme courts in the states and in the nation. For instance the eight-hour law for women, which as state factory inspector she had administered for a year, was declared unconstitutional by the Supreme Court of Illinois and she later saw the minimum wage measures which had been enacted into laws by state legislatures made inoperative because they were declared unconstitutional by the Supreme Court of the United States. This was true of an attempt to limit the hours of work for the bakers of New York State, of the minimum wage law for women in Oregon, and of similar legislation. Mrs. Kelley contended that this judicial nullification of beneficent legislation on the ground of unconstitutionality set a distinct limitation to the experiments through which the nation might increase its fund of social knowledge and that it curtailed the opportunity for utilizing experimentation as a method for progressive government. She pointed out that over and over again intelligent attempts to deal with a social evil, if made the basis of legal enactment, were less likely to receive judicial approval than an outworn method of dealing with the same evil which had the doubtful value of an early precedent under conditions long obsolete. She devoutly believed and was afterward upheld by Justice Holmes in minority opinions of Supreme Court decisions, that the process of adjustment to current conditions is a necessity if constitutional government is to endure.

In these discussions Julia Lathrop usually was found defending the actions of the courts, insisting that we must proceed by precedent broadening into precedent and she held to this during the very disappointing decision of the Supreme Court in regard to the constitutionality of the federal Child Labor law which she was then administering as chief of the Children's Bureau. It is fair to her changing position however to quote from a speech that she once made to the League of Women Voters:

> As citizens of the United States, whatever our differences of opinion, we have turned of late to our Declaration of Independence and to our Constitution with a new sense of their vitality. Some of us think the Constitution ought not to be touched but that like the ark it is a complete and finished vehicle of a sacred utterance. Others of us believe that the Constitution is a living testament of adaptations to the changes which are taking place in our country. All of us respect the patriotism, the courage and the statesmanship of the men who wrote it. Even those of us who have no legal training feel that human struggle to reach just agreements of which our Constitution is the result. Men of differing lives and characters and social traditions came together eleven years after the Declaration of Independence to try to find a way by which they could agree upon a joint expression of the essential principles on which they believed the union of the states must rest.

> They never thought they had written a perfect thing. They knew they had set up after many compromises the minimum framework of a common government. And it stands with repeated modifications after one hundred and fifty years of extraordinary national growth.

Julia Lathrop had long attended the sessions of the National Conference of Social Work, many of them when it was called the National Conference of Charities and Correction. Although in later years its delegates were not so largely representative of governmental institutions, a certain number of public officials registered in its membership every year with the thousands of citizens from every state in the Union who were engaged in all sorts of philanthropy. Graham Taylor thus describes its representative capacity: "The classes, occupations and interests best known by those who speak for them here are constituent elements of the nation as much as any congressman's district or constituents. Indeed there are many thousands of our population who are not represented anywhere else and have no other spokesmen than those who appear for them here. They are the dependent, defective and delinquent classes cared for by those who gather in this conference to learn from one another how better to care for them." She was profoundly interested that the state and county officials who attended the conference should be kept in close touch with the experiences and attitudes of the volunteer social workers and be pushed towards better administration of existing laws. She realized how easy it was to consider a given measure as secure when the government has taken it over but perhaps no one in the conference knew better than she how necessary it is that social workers should still feel interested in the measures they have advocated and should identify themselves with the officials charged with difficult and sometimes experimental administration. This attitude of hers occasionally appeared to the younger and ardent would-be sociologists in the conference like a throw-back to the old days of the Conference of Charities and Correction although it was greatly to the special interests of these young people that the measures they were thrusting into governmental agencies should be properly administered. Another reason why she was so deeply concerned for the development of public social service of a high professional standard was that only the public agency can be absolutely comprehensive and really continuous. The comprehensiveness was always a goal, for this meant that all who needed it were to be included in the service provided. On one occasion Florence Kelley spoke vigorously before a large general session of the National Conference of Social Work discussing methods of caring for widows and their children. "The thing to do for widows and orphans," she said quickly, "is to abolish them!"—and she went on speedily to laws concerning industrial accidents and workmen's compensation. Julia Lathrop of course agreed with her—she could always be trusted to take a large view of any situation,—but she warned the social workers at the conference that even such measures would not help the hard lot of the poor unless the officials in charge of administration knew actual conditions.

This desire to enrich and ennoble public service is to be found in practically all Julia Lathrop's speeches before the Conference. As late as 1930, when she was reporting on "What the Indian Service Needs," in the Boston Conference, she made an eloquent plea that social workers should consider governmental positions in the Indian Service. She quoted from President Masaryk—in the opinion of many, the wisest, most practical and most useful statesman in Europe—as follows: "One of the problems of Democracy is how to put true and noble human qualities into politics, and into the administration of the state."

In the same address she deplored that, while the Government statistical material is basic, it is unfortunate that the art of popularizing has not seemed of equal importance, and she ventured the belief "that nothing could be more valuable than that such skillful attention should be devoted to the interpretation of such reports, and addressed to the public by varying expedients."

Throughout Julia Lathrop's years in attendance at the conferences she was almost universally recognized as able to apply to perplexing social situations as they arose, the ability which can best be described as that of statesmanship. A host of her colleagues in social work would heartily agree with Graham Taylor's tribute: "Miss Lathrop was attracted to social work as a statesman, seeing in statesmanship a gigantic lever for wide social reform."

That Julia Lathrop was elected President of the National Council of Social Work in 1917 with the enthusiastic backing of all the young and radical members, demonstrated once again how thoroughly she and the young people understood each other.

The following extracts from her letters written to Florence Kelley reveal something of the range and continuity of their mutual interests. The first have to do with efforts to secure legislation:

April 28, 1923

This week we had our first bout with the Illinois legislature. You would be surprised a little I think to find the amount of mis-statement which is lavishly circulated among our best citizens especially among the ladies of high standing and which is in some cases lapped up as if it were wholesome. I do not know how we shall come out. I think the deep basic difficulty which paralyzes our effort lies in the bad political situation in our state as a whole, which has put into the hands of physicians responsibility not to their profession but to politicians who control the medical service of the state. It is a strange situation—perhaps it must last until the end of this administration. Perhaps we shall be beaten but I try to remember that lobbying is an alluring indoor sport if properly played.

I sat in the House while the vote was taken on the eight-hour bill, and saw Mrs. O'Neill's triumph borne so modestly that a person who did not know the English language would not have known that anything was happening to her. However there will be more trouble.

Oct. 4, 1926

If you all decide on the meeting in Washington I will come if it seems clear that I can help. Myself I doubt if I *could* be useful. While I have a few friendly connections I am ashamed to think of some legislators who detest me. It will not be easy for me to come but you know—or rather you cannot possibly know that my instinct is to do anything you ask, and I am not ready to refuse this although for various good personal reasons I earnestly hope it may prove undesirable for our purpose.

The next letters refer to international matters:

January 27, 1927

I think that I must go to the Child Welfare Committee[1] meeting in Geneva. There has been great dissatisfaction because it appeared that none of the Western Assessors or committee members are coming. Hence with my usual luck I seem to go. And then I believe in the Committee if it can be equipped for research and study. On the whole I am not sure that much ground was lost at the last session. In view of the whole situation the triumph of our cause was remarkable and leaves us a breathing space and a spark of life.

1. A sub-committee of the Commission on the Welfare of Children and Young Persons of the League of Nations of which Miss Lathrop was appointed an assessor by the Council of the League in 1925.

GENEVA, SWITZERLAND, May 2, 1927

Our news is so complete and prompt and competently set forth that if it were only factual we would be the best informed newspaper readers in the world. I do not think the European press is any more factual—.

I do not blame other countries for disliking us nor for failing to dissemble but one is too conscious of the feeling to make attendance at even such meetings as this, a pure joy. One finds valued friends of course and politeness, but the air is not too warm otherwise. When Alice comes I hope to have a little luncheon and ask Gertrud Baumer who is here—a fine mind and a cautious view of matters—, the able Japanese Mr. Ito, and others. The Child Welfare Committee *can* do wonders if it is allowed to, and with patience and wisdom it doubtless will.

From a letter written to Florence Kelley at the death of her daughter just after she had entered Smith College I venture to quote the following paragraphs:

September 30, 1905

I am sure from the brief words of your telegram that you must already find a solace in the fact of the swift unconsciousness and painlessness of Margaret's death. When I think of her as I saw her last, so beautiful, so charmingly maternal and whimsical with the little Greek baby at Hull-House, so proud of you and with such a gay independence at the same time, I can hardly imagine a daughter more perfectly filling your own ideal. That she has been yours all these growing years and had reached that wonderful youth which leads on the imagination of every older observer into an earthly paradise and that she remains to all of us forever young, forever fair—all this seems to me in itself a wonderful possession and joy.

November 11, 1931

Dearest F.K.—How could you have the heart to stay weeks and weeks in a hospital and never let me know! Only when I ask a silly favor of you do you order your precious eldest born to write me as to a thing of no consequence about which I *should* not have troubled you when you were in the best of health. . . . I have an uneasy feeling about any of our precious H.-H. society daring to be ill or anything, and not telling me.

Because I am afraid that in presenting these two brilliant women I have stressed their zeal too much and their grace too little, I am adding an article Julia Lathrop wrote for *The Survey* only a few weeks before her own death, revealing as to both of these good friends.

FLORENCE KELLEY—1859–1932

To those who read this inadequate page the name of Florence Kelley is well known. Many of you know her as a personal friend and feel for her an intimate affection and a deep respect. None of us can quite bear yet to speak of her as if she had gone away from this world which she so tenderly loved, and the more we consider what she has given to it the more we realize that she had exemplified a spirit and method of social study and social work in the full sense of the words which will survive as long as those who come after her desire to continue her efforts, not looking down meticulously for her footprints, but in her spirit, heads up, looking forward, as she would wish.

Some of you knew Florence Kelley in her childhood or perhaps you went to school with her. I had no such privilege but we know that she was born to a conventional and luxurious life in Philadelphia, her father, William D. Kelley, one of the ablest lawyers and most distinguished political leaders of his time; her mother of a fine Quaker family, a woman of an exceptionally gentle and retiring nature. Both must have seen with rare wisdom that this brilliant intellectual child was not of the stuff to be driven or led in the old way of education but rather that she must be helped to find her own path. Thus she received a formal education indeed, but one of exceptional interest and breadth which she pursued from school in Philadelphia to Cornell University whose door just then was opened to women—there she was graduated with a brilliant record and thence she went to the University of Zurich. And it should be added here that years later when she felt that for her work as chief state factory inspector in Illinois she needed more knowledge of law, she quietly entered the classroom of the Northwestern University Law School, took the required courses in her spare time and received her degree in 1894.

Mrs. Kelley was an accomplished linguist and fine translations stand to her credit. Of course she was a Phi Beta Kappa. She was always by taste and attainments genuinely a scholar, with a scholar's choice contempt for pretentious writing and thinking. She became absorbed in economic and social study, in the practical as well as the student's view of the labor problem, in public education as the only substitute for child labor and in all the aspects of the struggling advance toward a just social order.

I first met Mrs. Kelley when she came to Chicago in 1891. She at once became a resident of Hull-House where she lived during the eight crowded years she spent in Illinois. Her coming was timely and she helped from the first. Miss Addams and she understood each other's powers and worked together in the wonderfully effective way many of us well remember.

Soon a new opportunity opened. John P. Altgeld, who became governor of Illinois in 1893, was a man of great independence of thought and action and entirely on his own initiative, so far as I have been able to learn, he determined to appoint qualified women to various administrative and advisory positions in the state service. These appointments, carefully made and non-political, surprised everyone and gratified at least the women of the state. The most important and difficult place was that of chief factory inspector and for this position the governor selected Mrs. Kelley and as first assistant appointed Mrs. Alzina P. Stevens of Chicago, a well known leader in women's labor organizations. A legend exists to the effect that when the announcement of these two appointments was made someone remonstrated in a friendly way, saying that two such "big women" would never be able to work together, to which the governor replied, according to the legend: "If they are big enough for the job, they will get along together well enough." The event proved that the governor was right.

Mrs. Kelley, her assistant and staff, worked courageously and ably in enforcing the Illinois statute restricting the work of women and girls in manufacture to eight hours in one day and forty-eight hours in one week, but the statute was short-lived. In 1895 the Supreme Court of Illinois pronounced the provision unconstitutional.

Mrs. Kelley remained in Chicago at Hull-House, always doing whatever came to her hand, studying, writing, teaching, speaking, always stimulating, until she seemed an essential element of Chicago. But in 1899 she became general secretary of the National Consumers' League whose office was in New York and from that office she reached out across our country and beyond for the rest of her life.

In New York she lived for some years at the Nurses' Settlement with Miss Wald and there as in Hull-House she gave invaluable help.

It was from this settlement background in two cities that she drew much of her intimate knowledge of human-kind, her interest in working women, in children, in Negroes and in immigrants.

In Mrs. Kelley's book, "Some Ethical Gains Through Legislation," published in 1905, we find a plan for a United States commission for children whose scope and purpose was carried out in concise form in the Children's Bureau Act of 1912. Its passage was aided by such support from the settlements as perhaps few of us realize.

We all know how lavishly and modestly Mrs. Kelley gave herself, how faithfully she attended conventions and conferences and committees, speaking in that flute-like voice as if she was delighted to have the privilege, praising and stimulating others, asking nothing for herself. She gave herself so unsparingly that sometimes it seemed as if her life was too hard, but as I think now of her life I think she had much happiness. She was surrounded by friends known and unknown—she must have felt that. Always her mind to her a kingdom was. She must have had happiness in ruling it for the common good. More precious than all else she had her beloved family, her sons, her grandchildren. Yes, hers was a nobly rich and generous life. We know its influence must reach far beyond her day and ours.

9

The First Juvenile Court, 1899—Paris, 1900

✒ Hull-House was early obliged to consider an aspect of education having to do with the streets rather than the schools; the inevitable temptations of commercialized amusements, the difficulties of a blind-alley job, meaningless conflicts with the police, the different standards of conduct required by old-world parents and by young Americans. Julia Lathrop wrote of the conditions surrounding children of the nineties, as follows:

> The belief that childhood is the period for education and should be spent neither in idleness nor in labor was haltingly expressing itself in our child-labor laws and school laws. But a more baffling problem presented itself. It applied not to all children but only to a neglected minority—those who committed or were charged with offenses against the law. Their sufferings made an appeal to both common-sense and pity, while their menace to the order of the society which disregarded them could not permanently be ignored.
>
> In Illinois the popular confidence in institutional care for children was still great and institutions providing care for orphans and homeless children were fairly adequate. The industrial schools for dependent boys and for girls were obliged to receive many neglected children whose experiences had been so nearly criminal that their mingling with innocent children was undesirable; yet they necessarily mingled in these institutions. This was because offenses were minimized by the courts in order to commit to industrial schools and thus save the child from the sure demoralization of imprisonment.

Another miscarriage of justice was obvious and it was also un-
avoidable without great changes in the treatment of delinquent children. Children over ten years of age were arrested, held in the police stations, tried in the police courts. If convicted they were usually
fined and if the fine was not paid sent to the city prison. But often
they were let off because justices could neither tolerate sending children to the Bridewell nor bear to be themselves guilty of the harsh
folly of compelling poverty-stricken parents to pay fines. No exchange of court records existed and the same children could be in
and out of various police stations an indefinite number of times,
more hardened and more skilful with each experience.

A curious situation had arisen in regard to the industrial schools. In
her journeys through the state Julia Lathrop had often been distressed
when she encountered the careless disposal of dependent children by a
probate judge. Because the county paid a fixed monthly amount for
each child committed to an industrial school at least one county judge
when asked to commit some neglected children to such a school for dependents was reported to have said: "Oh, that will cost the county too
much. Let them run another year and you can send them to the state
school [for delinquents] and that will not cost the county anything."

In January 1925 Julia Lathrop addressed a large group of interested
people who met in Chicago in joint commemoration of the 25th anniversary of the first Juvenile Court and of the 15th anniversary of the
first Psychopathic Institute. She gave a remarkable description of the
mounting sense of compunction and the increasing consciousness of
the need of such a court, which led finally to the establishment of the
first Juvenile Court in the world in 1899, the very year that another new
court, the Court of International Conciliation and Arbitration, was established in The Hague. Julia Lathrop told of the efforts the Chicago
Woman's Club had made on behalf of helpless delinquent children.

Its club committees had done much to improve the decency of the
police stations and the jail. They secured women matrons; they
maintained for years until taken over by the county a school for boys
awaiting trial or serving sentence in the jail. They urged a truant
school and supported compulsory education. They were deeply concerned by the official indifference which made the John Worthy
School a disappointment to those who hoped it would aid in wiser

treatment of juvenile delinquents. However interest was only stimulated by defeats. The concern became more general. Judges and prison wardens and other officials, public-spirited physicians, lawyers and clergymen, settlements, the State Board of Charities, the State Federation of Clubs, the principal child-caring societies, the Bar Association, showed a common desire to help. For some years the State Board of Charities had been accumulating first hand information as to the conditions of children throughout the state who were in poorhouses or otherwise neglected. When the annual session of the Illinois State Conference of Charities was held in November 1898 it was plain that various state organizations were considering legislative proposals for the benefit of differing types of children.

The president of the Illinois Conference of Charities that year was Jenkin Lloyd Jones who had been Julia Lathrop's confrere on the Illinois Board of Charities, and between them they arranged a fine program on the Children of the State. The conference was addressed by authorities of national standing, among others by Mrs. Lucy L. Flower of Chicago who with Julia Lathrop was the moving spirit of the new Juvenile Court and by Mary M. Bartelme who much later became judge of the court but at that moment was acting as public guardian in Cook County. The members of the conference were fired with such enthusiasm that a committee emerging from the conference induced Judge Hurley, a jurist of distinction, to draft the Illinois Juvenile Court Act. Julia Lathrop wrote of the work of this committee which had the able assistance of the bar association, the press and the general public during its long weeks of convincing the Legislature: "If there were dissensions at any point in securing the passage of the bill, time has amiably obliterated them from my mind and I recall only an extraordinary degree of that cooperative work in a good cause for which the men and women of Chicago have long been distinguished."

The actual Juvenile Court was finally established. It was for some time housed in the county building and then in a building of its own erected by the city upon land paid for by the county. This building took care of the growing probation department and provided quarters for the detention home, the latter equipped with pleasant schoolrooms and a gymnasium so complete that the opponents of the bill called it a "swell boarding-school for boys."

The new building was situated just east of South Halsted Street diagonally across from Hull-House, and never was a social experiment watched with more anxious care than that with which Julia Lathrop followed its growth year by year. Because the judges, other officials and visitors to the court often lunched in the Hull-House Coffee House she had opportunity for many unofficial discussions as to the theory and practice of the court. Concerning one of the early and most able of these judges, Julian W. Mack, for many years since a judge of the United States Circuit Court, Julia Lathrop said: "Judge Mack gave up most complicated and interesting legal work in order that he might help with the children's court. How ably he did it! We look back with the greatest pleasure and a thrill of pride not only to his decisions but to the educational campaign which he conducted at that time in order that the Juvenile Court might be interpreted to the people." In this interpretation, Judge Mack always emphasized the rôle of the chancellor who historically stood before the king as a defender of the people. Judge Mack said of this function:

> Let me explain for the benefit of the layman just what the chancery power of the court means and just what it is that is new that has been brought into our civilization by the Juvenile Court Law. It is not a question of machinery at all. We have had courts from time immemorial. We had probation in some places; we had separate hearings for the child in some places; we had certain institutions for the children different from those of the adult. What we did not have was the conception that a child that broke the law was to be dealt with by the State as a wise parent would deal with a wayward child.

Perhaps the most striking result of the Juvenile Court was that brought about in the law court as such, where lawyers have for many years ranged themselves to prosecute and to defend a prisoner. There was almost a change in *mores* when the Juvenile Court was established. The child was brought before the judge with no one to prosecute him and with no one to defend him—the judge and all concerned were merely trying to find out what could be done on his behalf. The element of conflict was absolutely eliminated and with it, all notion of punishment as such with its curiously belated connotation.

It is impossible to record adequately Julia Lathrop's unflagging interest in the Juvenile Court and the many developments her active mind suggested directly and indirectly. Judge Mary Bartelme, the first woman judge of the court, under whom it developed most interestingly, says of her: "Her splendid mind and energies never ceased to be active in securing for childhood the finest and best opportunities possible and the inception of the Juvenile Court movement as well as its constant progress and improvement owes much to her untiring leadership and inspiration."

Julia Lathrop said in one of her addresses:

> Perhaps it is not out of place to remind ourselves that it has been clear from the beginning that the great business of this court is intimately involved in the most delicate and complicated questions of social life. The court cannot serve its end unless it is sustained by intelligent public interest and cooperation. Increasingly it becomes evident that social forces which can really lessen the number of children who appear before the Juvenile Court are creative and not repressive forces. Good and intelligent parents, homes of decent comfort and a community which consciously protects public health, recreation and education are true guarantees of normal childhood.

After the Juvenile Court was established there was of course still much work to be done. Of the immediate next step Mrs. Joseph T. Bowen writes:

> Mrs. Flower had formed a committee of citizens called the Juvenile Court Committee, with Miss Julia Lathrop as its first president. I succeeded her I think in 1900.
>
> The law provided for the establishment of a Juvenile Court and for the services of probation officers, but it made no provision for the salary of these officers nor did it provide for a place of detention although it specifically set forth that children were not to be confined in jails or police stations. The Juvenile Court Committee then raised the money for the salaries of the probation officers, beginning with five and ending with twenty-two. It called an educator of note, Mr. Henry W. Thurston, to be chief probation officer; it also paid an assistant chief probation officer and the salaries of one or two clerks in the court. During this time the probation of-

ficers were most carefully selected by the Juvenile Court Committee. They met frequently with members of the committee at Hull-House and we talked with them of their duties. We really knew absolutely nothing about such duties. There was no literature on juvenile courts at that time, nor on probation officers, and those of us who had the selecting of these officers had to fall back on our own knowledge of human nature.

The committee maintained a detention home where children could be kept, awaiting final disposition through the Juvenile Court. This was no light undertaking for the committee insisted upon a homelike atmosphere with no visible means of restraint and the kindly matron in charge certainly did not suggest the warden of a prison.

Julia Lathrop was greatly amused by an incident which showed that the detention home had in fact become so much a home for the boys that they even felt responsible for its upkeep. Mrs. Bowen tells the story as follows:

> On one occasion one of our best boys escaped from the Home. We were rather unhappy about it because we had given him certain privileges and he seemed a reliable boy. He returned at the end of the day, very triumphant, carrying in each hand several chickens tied by the legs, and he said, "I felt so sorry for you ladies. You seemed to have such a hard time raising money to feed us kids that I just went out to Mrs. Story's chicken yard and got these chickens for you." He was very much upset, and we felt almost apologetic to take the chickens away from him and return them to the rightful owner.

This Juvenile Court Committee, after the building was established and the County had taken over the first functions performed by them, reorganized as the Juvenile Protective Association whose activities have continued for thirty-five years. It has succeeded in establishing various safeguards for city youth often in spite of the inherent difficulties of philanthropic effort in the face of municipal indifference.

At the monthly board meetings of the association the trustees were often distressed to find that the same type of case and often the same children were brought into court over and over again for similar offenses. At last it was apparent that many of these children were psychopathic cases and they and other border line cases needed more skilled care than the most devoted probation officer could give them. One of the members of the board, Mrs. William F. Dummer, guaranteed an adequate sum for the purpose of establishing a psychopathic clinic and for its maintenance for five years. This clinic was not only the beginning of the Illinois Institute for Juvenile Research, but the first of those clinics which have gradually extended to many courts for juveniles and to a few courts dealing with adults.

Julia Lathrop, chairman of a committee for securing a head for the new undertaking, interviewed both practicing alienists and also psychologists in several universities. When Dr. William Healy was selected she hoped that a practitioner accustomed to handling children "bare handed," as she said, would come to regard them as the family physician naturally regards his young patients. Dr. Healy served for eight years in Chicago as head of the ever-growing psychopathic clinic, first under the auspices of the committee and then under the County itself. Later he went to Boston and is now head of the Judge Baker Guidance Center.

Dr. Healy writes of the beginnings of the first psychopathic clinic as follows:

> As I remember it, the steps which led to the organization of the Institute were about as follows: In 1908 we had some talk about it, following some lectures which I gave at the School of Civics. Then I made a trip about the country trying to find out what others knew about the possibilities of such an organization. I gained very little information, but did receive much encouragement.
>
> Miss Lathrop told me that it was a talk that she had with William James which induced her to argue for my taking over the project myself. Then came Mrs. Dummer's offer to finance the undertaking for five years, and I gave up my private practice for the sake of the new venture. We began work in April, 1909, in the old Juvenile Detention Home. Miss Lathrop was very helpful in every practical sense and at first entered into some of our schemes and then decided it was not her field and afterwards acted only in an occasional advisory capacity.
>
> Very few meetings of the Organization were ever held after the first ones. It really was blazing a new trail and there were no other

clinics to pattern after. Miss Lathrop's main contribution, as I look back upon it, was in helping with matters of policy. . . . Miss Lathrop's wisdom and unusual practical sense was always a tremendous help. I don't think there were any particular dissensions in points of view among the early advisers, and that was probably due to the fact that no one had any experience in the field and perhaps even more largely due to Miss Lathrop's firmly guiding hand. Everyone was willing to co-operate. She very evidently felt, and I believe definitely stated, that it was best that the Institute be left alone to see what it could discover. She aided and abetted in every way the development of those first researches which led to the publication of "The Individual Delinquent." So far as the working of the Institute was concerned, it was very smooth sailing for me and my assistants.

Miss Lathrop stands out for me as a vivid personality, characterized not only by great kindliness, but also with peculiarly shrewd insight and much practical wisdom.

It is also in connection with this first Juvenile Court that I recall an example of her indulgence to human weakness which was as always not only kindly but amusingly rational. In this instance she was able to extend such indulgence to pretentious "claims for credit," which is perhaps the most difficult field in which to exercise it.

One evening upon my return from the committee arranging for celebration of the 25th anniversary of the Juvenile Court, when we had been solemnly assured by one woman after another that she herself had been really instrumental in securing the court, I said to Julia Lathrop that as chairman of the committee I had the honor officially to inform her that every woman in Cook County except Mrs. Flower and herself had been personally responsible for the existence of the court. To this Julia Lathrop replied that in a sense it was true, that the court could not have been secured without the backing of thousands of women, and, with a suspicious twinkle, she added that if each one of these women felt personally responsible for it, the demonstration was complete that the court was well entrenched in the mother heart of Cook County; as if for good measure, she concluded that we all had long recognized the sense of possession as a familiar manifestation of maternal affection.

The Juvenile Court always remained in her mind as an important social institution. Years after her long experience in the Children's Bureau, Catherine I. Hackett who interviewed her one May morning in New York as she ate her breakfast on the balcony of the clubhouse of the American Association of University Women, reports her as saying:

> Anyone who has studied the children brought into juvenile courts realizes that a large part of juvenile delinquency is due to grinding poverty. It is at the basis of our social problem. I believe that within fifty years we can make a start toward abolishing poverty—the social worker sees already definite attacks being made on poverty and by paths so direct that they are unavoidable. . . . The drive against poverty will go on with increasing momentum as the public is educated to the importance of abolishing it through state action. This is a move based upon economics and not upon sentiment.

Julia Lathrop of course was active in her help to secure the Mothers' Pension Act administered by the Juvenile Court in the interest of the dependent child. She was enormously absorbed in the addition of a vocational bureau to the public schools system, equipped with a staff of visiting teachers, and of course also in the provisions for public recreation afforded by the growing system of playgrounds and small parks. She believed in the public administration of children's affairs provided always that the system could be kept free from self-seeking, and she constantly urged women to bestir themselves on behalf of the children.

In the meantime she worked constantly in voluntary organizations, was a trustee of the Elizabeth McCormick Fund, and identified with almost every child-caring agency in Illinois.

In June 1900 I was appointed a juror in social economics of the Paris Exposition. It was the first time that the term Social Economics had been officially used in relation to an exhibit at a World's Fair and we were naturally much interested in it both as to what would be exhibited and as to how social economics could be visualized. Julia Lathrop who had previously studied the care of the insane in Scotland as well as the remarkable care accorded to them in the village system centered at Gheel in Belgium, had long been planning to see the care of epileptics as carried on at Bielefeld in Westphalia. I was more than happy when she decided to go to Paris with me. It turned the entire affrighting situation into one of confidence and adventure.

We found the social economics department housed in a charming white wooden building which had been erected on the exposition grounds by the French Trade Unions without the intervention of a contractor or other business supervision. We were both enormously interested I remember in the housing exhibit especially in the provisions made in various countries that working men might own their homes. We had both grown a little skeptical of the wisdom of a workingman putting his savings into a house and thereby losing his "mobility of labor" when a crisis might arise such as we had experienced in 1893. We recalled one of our old friends at Hull-House, who when the factory in which he was a skilled foreman had moved to Indiana could not follow his work away from Chicago because he could not dispose of his house and never since had been able to secure an adequate job. We therefore were delighted when we found the exhibit of the Belgian plan by which a man might begin to pay the government in monthly instalments for a house in Brussels but if midway in the process he found it advantageous to move to Ghent he could transfer his payments to a similar house which the government would sell him there.

When we arrived in Paris we found a cable stating that Mrs. Stevens had died at Hull-House. She was one of our most vigorous residents, Florence Kelley's deputy inspector for Illinois and later the first probation officer of the Juvenile Court. Alzina Parsons Stevens was born in New England at the time when children there were permitted to enter the factories at any age when they were considered useful. She had gone into a textile factory at the age of nine and had promptly lost two fingers of her right hand because she was too little to reach up to the power loom and too ignorant to understand the dangers of oiling the cogged wheels while they were in motion. She remained in the mills during the period characterized by the publication of "The Lowell Offering" and similar pamphlets when these young girls and even the children followed the New England tradition of recording their reflections on life and its strange mutations. Mrs. Stevens was always enthusiastic over the spirit and ability of those early mill workers who like Lucy Larcom herself had no notion that there could be any difference between their interests and the interests of their employers. Through her long life in the labor movement, and she was one of the first women to be admitted to the Typographical Union, she looked back to this beginning of women's work in factories as a halcyon experience in spite of her own crippling injury. She was for many years a friend of Eugene Debs, and during a crisis in the Pullman strike gave him haven in her suburban home until he could once more assume control of a difficult strike situation, an episode characteristic of the strategy she had learned in long experience in the labor movement.

Julia Lathrop and I in our mutual sense of loss in the death of Mrs. Stevens spoke often that summer of the deeper issues of life and death.

Paris was filled with American and English people as well as continentals drawn not only to the exposition but to the international conferences of various sorts which were being held there, notably the International Council of Women and a dissenting group of radical feminists. One afternoon we attended a meeting of these militant suffragists. We were seated solemnly upon the platform in a group of American women, all there in the capacity of visitors, and we listened in proportion as our knowledge of French permitted, to an animated discussion of the unfairness to women of the Napoleonic code still in large measure operative in France. This code gave the full custody of a child over six years old absolutely to the father and the child's mother had no legal redress, whatever her husband decided to do. Suddenly the somewhat dreary recital was broken into by a flow of Gallic eloquence which filled the hall with amplitude and power. The leading woman lawyer in France told what women were driven to do in order to avoid such an unfair situation. Her own father and mother living in unbroken marital relations to the end of their lives had never been legally married because they both felt they should have mutual direction of the lives of their children. An unmarried woman had of course complete control of her child as, theoretically at least, the state did not know who was her child's father under the rule of *la recherche de la paternité interdite.* The orator stated expressly that her own two children had been born out of wedlock although she and their father observed all the conventions of marriage save the legal tie. She argued that a legal code so unfair to women inevitably drove them into such a position.

Suddenly there was a stir among the group of American women on the platform and an imposing matron whispering in my ear that of course we could not countenance such talk as this, impressively left the hall followed by all of her fellow-countrywomen save Julia Lathrop seated at one end of the row and myself at the other. We were a little disconcerted for a moment and certainly we were made uncomfortably conspicuous. As we left the hall after the stirring session had ended in a wild debate between the two points of view, trying to change the law by legal process or through defying it, I launched a query to Julia Lathrop as to how Mrs. X could have left the discussion at such an exciting moment. She replied, "Mrs. X doesn't really care about the legal relation of women to their children but she is enormously interested in her own dignity and what she calls her 'influence on others'. It is a terrible handicap and of course she will never learn much about anything as long as she lives." Julia Lathrop may have felt that she was unjustly severe with a well meaning woman, or it may be that her fertile mind at once saw the dangers of the reverse practice, for she went on to speak of one of those irrational outcomes of human conduct always so unexpected—that the reformer resenting the wrongs of the common man and pleading the cause of the people because of their need and not because of their virtues, easily finds himself among the self-righteous where he can do nothing more for his cause and he too can learn nothing more.

When I settled down to the business of being a juror Julia Lathrop went on to visit the famous epileptic colony in Germany, but in August we crossed the Atlantic together homeward bound on a huge boat carrying many immigrants. The journey was marked by an incident characteristic of Julia Lathrop. Only seldom did she show a trace of that indignation which the abuse and neglect of the helpless so easily arouses; and as usual she kept herself in hand, if only because she needed the use of all her faculties and in her own words she "felt no call to dissipate them." The coarse black bread which was given the immigrant passengers to eat with their coffee in the morning, with their stew at noon, and again with their coffee at night, had been stowed on the ship while it was still hot so that it had become filled with a green mould which made it certainly unpalatable and probably dangerous. A committee of desperate immigrants who had complained in vain to lesser officials, finally made their way to the captain's bridge holding samples of the green bread in their hands. Unfortunately the burly captain was so enraged by this indignity and breach of ship discipline that he almost threw the panic stricken petitioners into the sea. During the next hour the complaint and samples of the bread reached Julia Lathrop, who took up the matter and by that wonderful method of hers which people call diplomacy but which was really a technique founded upon an understanding of human nature, by evening had secured the promise from the Captain himself that fresh bread should be baked for the immigrants every day. The steerage of course found out who was responsible for the new bread and it became embarrassing for her to walk on the deck because she was so frequently pointed out by the immigrants below, and when thoroughly identified was greeted with a volley of polyglot cheers.

10

School of Civics and Philanthropy, 1901— National Committee for Mental Hygiene, 1908–1909

✍ Because she was inevitably dissatisfied with the limited intelligence, of many of the attendants for the insane in the state hospitals, Julia Lathrop carried on a long struggle throughout her life to secure for such attendants some degree of training and the beginning of professional standards. Her help was eagerly welcomed by young alienists in the state institutions who were often working under great difficulties. This determination led her to arrange classes for the attendants at the new Chicago School of Civics and Philanthropy, founded by Dr. Graham Taylor, in which she had so large a part and where she saw a beginning of occupational therapy.

Dr. Alice Hamilton gives this estimate of the training thus established:

> What the American Medical Association called "a novel and interesting educational experiment" was the summer course for attendants in institutions for the insane which Julia Lathrop induced the Chicago School of Civics and Philanthropy to offer in 1908. This course was to include practical training in occupational therapy, then almost unknown in most state asylums, as well as lectures on mental disease and its treatment. Miss Lathrop in urging it painted a picture of the typical insane ward, "the rows of cleanly dressed patients seated in absolute idleness for hours together, their attendants satisfied with supplying their bodily needs and making no effort to rouse and stimulate them," and of the no less discouraging "restless ward, where so long as the patients give no serious trouble they

are left quite without direction for their activities." The character of the asylum she insisted depended on the character of the attendant, but then characteristically she went on to show how little chance an attendant had to be anything but a cog in a machine. "It is a strenuous, joyless and singularly isolated life. Such an institution is usually a little world in itself and the ideas and changing views of the outside world are slow in penetrating. Routine rules supreme, with all its warping and deadening influence."

Dr. Graham Taylor, the founder of the school, says of Julia Lathrop's identification with it: "The lack of trained workers in public institutions and in all social work led her to take part in initiating the Chicago School of Civics and Philanthropy as one of the first teachers."

She and Dr. Taylor were staunch friends and fellow-workers during those first years after the establishment of the school. The financial problem was always with the trustees and inevitably the entire undertaking was regarded as highly experimental. Dr. Taylor has said of her:

> She had the capacity to flank political opposition and exploitation rather than defeat by frontal attack. While politic in the best sense of the word, she was always direct in facing the issue. While tactful, she never compromised principles. In all exacting positions and situations she took her citizenship seriously. She was never impersonally official nor officially personal. The county's cases were her neighbors at Hull-House. The state's cases were her own wards. The nation's children and their mothers were her own heritage and hope in the American commonwealth.

Dr. Taylor has also said: "To her influence was due the establishment of its research department by the Russell Sage Foundation, mainly because she was to be its first Director."

Julia Lathrop, on June 1, 1907, wrote to Mr. John Glenn of the Russell Sage Foundation, as follows:

> I am delighted on sound principles to learn, since I returned from an especially unknowing six months abroad, that you are one of the Sage Fund trustees. Also since talking over with Dr. Graham Taylor this week the affairs of the Chicago Institute, I am glad that his application is in the hands of at least one person who will appreciate its importance to this part of the country. I have watched

with much admiration the patience and unselfishness with which Dr. Taylor has carried the really inordinate burden of the Institute. Its success has been such as to justify him, of course, but I have felt that the undertaking should have some financial basis which he was not directly responsible for. I need not say that I trust you and your associates will decide to aid in furnishing that basis.

Just now we are having a real revival of interest in public humanitarian work, although there have been tempestuous times in our legislature. We have state and county civil service laws which really demand the sort of training which the Institute should give. I think this a very promising and important matter for the Middle West—this of training for public service. I once hoped that the University of Illinois would give it but I see no prospect save the Institute. Please don't misunderstand this inquiry, by which I mean don't think it improper; however you must answer!

Six weeks later she wrote to Mr. Glenn again:

> I enclose some memoranda as to possible lines of study in Chicago. I have not had the time to do more nor indeed does it seem to me that you are likely to desire greater volume at any rate.
>
> I have wired Dr. Taylor to-day that I will undertake the directorship in charge of the research. I really think that I care a great deal about having a good center as a part of the Institute and as a part of Chicago's activity.
>
> Should it come about that I had the duty of directing all this, it would be a great honor and pleasure if only I can do the work. As to that I feel solemn doubts.
>
> I do not feel competent without further examination to make any statement as to the exact sums required for each inquiry submitted. I am sure that it would be unwise and thoroughly disappointing to undertake what he did not have money enough to carry through adequately.
>
> It was of course almost a foregone conclusion that the first of the "Suggestions as to Practicable Lines of Inquiry in Chicago," should be:
>
> I. *Inquiry into the causes of insanity,* emphasizing especially the social history and economic aspects of each case. At the present juncture Chicago offers peculiarly favorable opportunity for such study, which as far as I can learn has never been made.

Not only would the investigation be of genuine value *per se* but at this time the inquiry would give an impetus to important improvements in methods of first commitment and true hospital care in the Middle West, at least.

I am well assured that the authorities both medical and governmental in Chicago and in Illinois would welcome such an inquiry. The number of nationalities represented among the insane received at the Detention Hospital in Chicago would render the social study especially interesting and valuable.

There were also other suggestions, in regard to results of juvenile probation, various problems of women in industry followed by the last one: "If an intensive study of typical industrial districts in cities somewhat after the manner of Booth and Rowntree is to be undertaken, I think Chicago would afford especially illuminating material since she has various cosmopolitan quarters with population stable as compared with cities which are ports of entry."

The letter was in line with her genuine interest, for I recall Julia Lathrop's experience one spring when she accompanied Dr. Alice Hamilton through Illinois towns whose darker aspects were already so familiar to both of them. At my request Dr. Hamilton has written the following account of a tour of inspection she made for the Illinois Commission on Occupational Diseases of which Prof. Charles Henderson of the University of Chicago was chairman. The journey took place soon after the horrible Cherry Mine disaster which occurred in 1909 when Julia Lathrop was still a member of the Illinois State Board of Charities. She had therefore been concerned with a philanthropic machinery set in motion to care for the victims of the disaster. Following the heroic efforts of the Red Cross and other volunteer agencies the legislature finally appointed the Illinois Mining Investigation Commission of which Dr. Graham Taylor of the Chicago Commons was a member. The commission in fixing the responsibility for the disaster, described it as "pitifully preventable." Dr. Hamilton writes:

In the spring of 1910 Julia Lathrop made a trip through the lead centers of southwestern Illinois and of the St. Louis region with me, for at that time I was supervising an investigation of the poisonous trades of Illinois for Governor Deneen's Commission on

Occupational Diseases of which I was a member. At that time almost nobody admitted the responsibility of society and of the employing class for the accidents and diseases of industrial workers and most employers still insisted that it was up to the working man to protect himself and that only the deliberately careless ever came to harm. This pleasant theory was easy to hold because there was then no compensation for injury to a workman through dust or poisons, therefore the employer did not have those painful incidents forced on his attention.

On that trip Julia Lathrop saw men making white lead and red lead in atmospheres thick with poisonous dust, she saw men on blast furnaces forced to breathe deadly lead fumes, and she heard employers and plant physicians assure us that if the men would only wash their hands they would not get poisoned. Partly it was genuine ignorance, but partly it was the perfectly natural desire to quiet an uneasy conscience. One employer stood out from the crowd, Frank Hammar of East St. Louis, who with nobody to guide him but a tragically ignorant physician as struggling to make his white lead plant safe to work in. But for the most part little account was taken of the hordes of Negroes and poor whites from "Egypt" and the Ozarks and Arkansas, who drifted in and out of the plants, with no effort made to lessen the enormous overturn, indeed the more humane foremen told us that they encouraged it, believing that it was better to get rid of the men before they got too seriously poisoned. That was the sole measure of protection in some plants, we found.

We went to the homes of sick workmen to hear their side of the story and there we found the same attitude. Lead poisoning was something for which the worker was responsible although, like original sin, there seemed to be no way for him to escape it. In one house we found an Italian workman recovering from "lead fits," the cerebral form of lead poisoning, now very rare, then only too familiar to all smelter and white lead men. He had got over the delirium and convulsions but he was a pallid, tremulous wreck quite unfit to do any work, it seemed, for months to come. He told us the history of his illness and when I asked, "But why did you keep on after you knew the lead had got you?" he answered, "Well, there was the wife and the kids and we were paying on the house." I looked at the bleak, ugly house and at the two youngsters, both bleary-eyed with colds in their heads and badly in need of handkerchiefs, and it seemed to me that the price paid for his treasures was almost too high. But Julia's comment was: "What a terrible thing, to exploit the finest things in a man, his love of family, his sense of responsibility and his capacity for sacrifice, all to make white paint!"

Of course white lead paint can be produced without any such ruthless exploitation and nowadays it is, but only a quarter of a century ago our experience in those lead towns could have been repeated over and over. They made a deep impression on Julia Lathrop.

This early school of philanthropy was later taken over by the University of Chicago and has become a graduate professional school for the "social worker" being the same relation in kind although not yet in degree, to the graduate students as the professional schools of law and medicine. The present dean of the Graduate School of Social Service Administration of the University of Chicago, Dr. Edith Abbott, who also knew Julia Lathrop as a fellow resident at Hull-House, has written so convincingly in the following article published in the School's *Social Service Review,* that I am quoting from it in some detail. It is entitled, "Julia Lathrop and the Public Social Services."

> To all of those who worked with her in the numerous and various social undertakings which her resourceful and fertile mind and heart originated, Julia Lathrop was not only leader but friend. More than twenty years ago Julia Lathrop and Miss Breckinridge of the University of Chicago, who was then associated with her in the old School of Civics and Philanthropy, came to Wellesley College where I was then teaching Economics, and invited me to join with them in the establishment of what should be called a social research department or a department of social investigation in the School of Civics and Philanthropy which was then being reorganized in Chicago.
>
> I gladly accepted the invitation, although older members of Wellesley faculty considered it an indication of a mild form of lunacy for anyone to leave Wellesley College for an unheard of place called a school of civics and philanthropy. But I knew that a new "road to freedom" had been opened for me and I replied to all questions that I much preferred a new educational undertaking with Miss Lathrop and Hull-House to teaching in any women's college anywhere. I found, as I had expected to find, that Miss Breckinridge and I were quite free in working out new plans and methods of de-

veloping social research in a way that should relate such work very closely to the professional interests of social workers and also in the way that would make social research an integral part of pro fessional education for such work.

Miss Lathrop, through her long years of service on the Illinois State Board of Charities, had a large vision regarding social work and the confusing and limited attempts that were being made to give people the varied forms of service they so greatly needed. Through Miss Lathrop our Chicago School became thoroughly committed to the principle that adequate service could come only through establishing public social service on a high level. She wanted an educated and scientifically trained group in the public social services as fast as they could be established. She was never afraid of new ventures and with her help we worked out the plan for that early course given by Dr. William Healy in the School, a course that he called "Mental and Physical Factors in Dependency and Delinquency," which was I believe the first course in social psychiatry in any school of social work.

The social research undertakings that we initiated at the old school as well as those we have later carried on were also influenced by her interest in the public social services. She wrote the introduction to our first study of the Cook County Juvenile Court for a book called "The Delinquent Child and the Home," which was published by the Russell Sage Foundation. This introductory statement was, like so many of the things she wrote, prepared with great care and a warm interest in the subject. I consider it an historic statement of early Juvenile Court history, for in that introduction Miss Lathrop described conditions in the children's section of the House of Correction before the establishment of the Juvenile Court, when little children were committed for the non-payment of fines. At her request one of our graduate students, William L. Chenery, who was then a resident of Hull-House and is now editor of *Collier's Weekly,* went out to the House of Correction and copied the records of the six months preceding the establishment of the Juvenile Court. Miss Lathrop therefore had an exact statement of what happened to children before this new and great change of which the Juvenile Court had become the symbol had taken place in the relation of the State and its children. To the end of her life she was deeply concerned about the development of the Juvenile Court. She was delighted with the plans made to establish a merit system in the Chicago court and rejoiced over the fine and competent staff of officers secured.

After she became Chief of the Children's Bureau she made it possible for us to carry on some other juvenile court studies which appeared later as Children's Bureau publications. . . . It was also at her suggestion that we began a series of housing studies here in Chicago and she approved of the publication of these studies as magazine articles or in any other way that made them easily available and likely to yield useful, practical results. She was also interested in the early studies of working certificates and child labor which finally led to the publication by the University of Chicago Press of a book called "Truancy and Non-Attendance in the Chicago Schools," out of which finally developed the department of Vocational Guidance in the public schools and the so-called visiting teacher work.

To Miss Lathrop we owe our staunch belief in the importance of social research as a sound means of social reform. She supported us in rejecting the academic theory that social work could be "scientific" only if it had no regard to the finding of socially useful results and no interest in the human beings whose lives were being studied. The School of Social Service Administration of the University of Chicago acknowledges with deep humility and gratitude the leadership and constructive help given by Julia Lathrop over a period of nearly a quarter of a century.

It was seven years after the founding of this early school of social work that a nation-wide organization, the Mental Hygiene Society, was formed. All during those seven years Julia Lathrop had the condition of the insane constantly on her mind, had aroused an increased interest on their behalf and had advocated much needed reforms in the methods employed in their care. She had therefore an absorbing interest in the organization of the Mental Hygiene Society. For years she had been distressed over the number of people coming to Hull-House on various errands who were evidently psychopathic cases, many of them in wretched need of skilled services but not necessarily of hospitalization if their families could be instructed to care for them. She also knew other cases in the hospitals for the insane who could have been sent home if their families could be assured of medical guidance. She therefore dreamed of a society composed of visiting nurses trained to give psychiatric care under the professional direction of alienists to those two types of cases. She also believed that such nursing would come to have a preventive effect such as had been achieved by the societies for the care of tuberculosis.

She was greatly interested in Clifford Beers' book with a preface by William James entitled, *The Mind That Found Itself*, which was published in March 1908, and in the society which Mr. Beers inaugurated in New Haven in the following May. Lillian D. Wald, who with Julia Lathrop attended a meeting of the Connecticut society, gives a moving description of Julia Lathrop's almost unendurable sense of relief and her touching gratitude that such an effort had at last been organized. Her usual calm gave way and as she came out from the meeting her face was wet with tears.

The society grew rapidly beyond its original state dimensions and Mr. Beers advocated "the formation of a National Committee for Mental Hygiene which would be equally the friend of the physician and the patient; also the friend of a patient's relatives to whom, when burdened with an actual or impending affliction, it would become an unfailing source of information, advice and comfort. In a word, it would be a friend to Humanity, for no man knows when he himself may have to look for assistance." It was almost inevitable that Julia Lathrop should attend the organization of this national committee which met at New York in February 1909. The short preamble begins as follows: "We, the founders of The American Foundation for Mental Hygiene, are met upon the effort to create and carry forward a means effective to the end of promoting and conserving mental health and ameliorating the scourge of mental ill health."

The twelve charter members present at the Founding Meeting of the National Committee for Mental Hygiene were: Dr. Llewellys F. Barker, Prof. Russell H. Chittenden, Horace Fletcher, Dr. August Hoch, Prof. William James, Marcus M. Marks, Dr. Adolf Meyer, Dr. Frederick Peterson, Dr. Jacob Gould Schurman, the Rev. Anson Phelps Stokes, Jr., Miss Julia C. Lathrop and Clifford W. Beers.

The Mental Hygiene Society was formally organized in 1909, the very same year in which the first psychopathic clinic was established at the Juvenile Court of Chicago. Julia Lathrop must have felt that year that the inertia and public indifference as to mental handicaps were at last breaking up.

Upon her return to Chicago from the initial meeting of the National

Committee she was naturally active in the organization of the Chicago branch of the Mental Hygiene Society. The society has had an honorable career and is still usefully functioning in Chicago. Julia Lathrop was always especially grateful to Mrs. William S. Monroe who stood by the society through its darkest days, as well as to the group of distinguished alienists so responsible for its usefulness. She must have felt a thrill of satisfaction when during the War the society which had made itself responsible for the Favill School of Occupational Therapy, constantly sent advanced students to work with the insane and feeble-minded in the County Infirmary and with the patients in the County Hospital as well as with those in the state institutions. Such teaching has become part of the permanent services rendered in all these places. Her friend Mrs. George Dean recalls a committee meeting of the Mental Hygiene Society when after a Sunday supper at Mrs. Henrotin's house a few people continued to talk together in that intimacy which sometimes descends even upon a committee meeting. Each one was telling what she would rather do if she were free from all restrictions and obligations and could do exactly what she wanted to. Mrs. Henrotin said she would like to give all her time to defeating for reelection a certain Illinois congressman who was constantly blocking her most cherished schemes; Julia Lathrop said, with that deliberate enunciation which she sometimes used when speaking the "solemn truth," that what she would like best of all to do, would be to keep a boarding house for the insane. The incident may have occurred shortly after her investigation of the village care of the insane in Belgium where she had been so pleased to find the insane treated like other people. She induced her friend and fellow resident Alice Hamilton to write in the *Journal of the American Medical Association* on the need of psychopathic training for students in the medical schools, but they were both much disappointed three years later, after they had assumed that the movement was making remarkable progress, when Dr. Hamilton, asking a scientific librarian for material on the subject, was handed back her own article as all that the library possessed.

We all remember Julia Lathrop's endless kindness to individual patients. One of the Hull-House residents, Clara Landsberg, was much interested in the family of a Bohemian tailor. The poor man fell into melancholia and was sent to the wards of the hospital for the insane, then still maintained as part of the Cook County Infirmary at Dunning. In spite of his abstraction he was very unhappy especially over the institutional clothing, ill-cut and ill-fitting, so unlike the clothes he had always been able to make for himself. When after three months he seemed worse rather than better, Clara Landsberg appealed to Julia Lathrop to have him removed to a state institution. The judge before whom the petition was made, objected that the County had very little money and it would be too expensive to move him. Julia Lathrop in her very reasonable and conciliatory way finally convinced him that if Miss Landsberg paid the cost of transportation for the patient and his escort from Dunning to Kankakee, the County need have no expense. Miss Landsberg herself took him to the state hospital accompanied by the friendly police officer detailed at Hull-House, who was in civilian dress, and the patient never associated him with the party. Julia Lathrop remarked that such a friendly escort was the only proper method of taking a patient to a state institution, and she was much pleased that the patient began to improve almost immediately after his transfer and was shortly restored to his family.

Another resident, Dr. James A. Britton, recalls that late one evening Julia Lathrop received a message from the Harrison Street police station that a woman who was insane had been "run in" and was spending the night in a cell with the "drunks." Dr. Britton procured a hansom cab as the quickest thing available and went with her to the police station. They found the woman, who was obviously insane, in a room with three drunken men. Julia Lathrop was very much disturbed that the police should have made such a mistake for by that time orders had been given that cases of even suspected insanity were to be taken directly to the psychopathic hospital. The police were rather alarmed by her charges and immediately handed the woman over to her. The patient was added to the passengers in the cab and taken at once to the hospital. Dr. Britton was much impressed by the vigor and efficiency of the entire undertaking.

Throughout the years since its foundation, the Society for Mental Hygiene has established its branches or their prototypes in every country in the civilized world. Dr. Adolf Meyer, whom Julia Lathrop knew and admired in his first professional position, has long been the chairman of the advisory committee on psychiatric education and has been largely responsible for the extension of a most useful function of the society.

Possibly Julia Lathrop's unflagging interest in the mental hygiene movement may have been founded upon her remarkable capacity to evoke a sympathetic response from the most unpromising human mind. Certainly I never knew but one other person who was so willing "to suffer fools gladly" as Julia Lathrop was. She would give hours of unflagging sympathy and attention to the most unprepossessing caller who wished to talk to her. I passed through Hull-House lounge one afternoon and saw her in conversation with a well known visitor who notoriously lacked both good sense and sincerity. We had evolved a series of little signals at Hull-House by which we called for help when in dire need of release from just such a situation as this but Julia Lathrop paid no attention to my wigwagging and I crossed the hall into the library to overhear two residents conversing about the matter. The first one declared that it was a great waste for as valuable a person as Julia Lathrop to spend so much time with such an obvious fool, to which the second resident replied that she felt we had missed the whole point of the conversation, that Julia Lathrop had reduced the woman to a simpler state of mind than she had probably felt since her childhood and that she was for the moment talking directly and sincerely. The resident then added, "If the psychiatric social workers would learn to do that, they would be worth their salt but I have never seen anyone else with or without psychiatric training who could accomplish it; it is the very essence of psychoanalysis stripped of all its technical and laborious processes. Mrs. X will leave here refreshed and rejuvenated and will never know what has happened to her. She will try to explain it by calling Miss Lathrop a wonderful person." I added as a fervent *amen* to the little sermon, "Which the same she certainly is!"

11

With Women's Organizations— Immigrants' Protective League

🖎 Julia Lathrop was the most stimulating and great-hearted of friends not only to individuals but to groups of people as well. She would lend her whole mind, the endless resources of her rich experience to a given situation which might be facing Hull-House or another group to which she held her allegiance. She possessed the devotion of friendship itself for organization and for even units of government which most people are able to extend only to individuals. This amazing capacity humanized every social situation and kept her intelligence free from that attitude which has been described by an American journalist as "much more interested in affirming ideals than in facing the problems of applying them."

An interesting discussion club is described by Judge Mary Bartelme as follows:

> The Everyday Club was a group of forty civic minded women who met at luncheon whenever called together by a committee of three to discuss current topics when in the opinion of the committee an interesting matter was before the public. Among the members were Mrs. Fannie Bloomfield Zeisler, Mrs. Charles Henrotin, Mrs. Ella Flagg Young, Mrs. Henry Frank, Miss Addams and others. Women who were fortunate enough to be members will always rejoice in the memory of Julia Lathrop's fine clear discussion of any subject in which she took part and her able summing up of the best and most direct way to proceed to accomplish or correct conditions according to their needs.

Julia Lathrop was at her best, perhaps, at such gatherings where her always keen mind was stimulated to its most alert expression. Such clear thinking on the part of one person has an enormous liberating power and taps new sources of energy in others. The result of a generous and fearless desire to see life as it is, irrespective of the confines and limitations which so needlessly divide it, can only be obtained at its best in a group of friends such as the Everyday Club became.

Her identification with women's organizations which went back into the 1890's when as a long-time member of the State Board of Charities she constantly needed their help for improving the state institutions is thus described by one of her friends as the days "before we had the Juvenile Court and when women were just becoming aroused to a sense of responsibility toward those whom we call deficient, dependent and delinquent, when Julia Lathrop was the inspiration to sane, fine action resulting in changed conditions in many of our institutions." She never grew too solemn about it all as the members of the early women's clubs were somewhat prone to do in their first efforts at public service. I recall in the nineties at a hearing on child labor before a committee of the Illinois Legislature when one of the politicians, utilizing the well worn joke about old maids' children, asked her how many children she had raised, that Julia Lathrop without a moment's hesitation and yet with no suggestion of a retort but as if she were answering a commonplace question replied, "With a little help from my father and mother I have raised four."

Lillian Wald tells of a conference on day nurseries held in the Charities Building in New York where a point was made by several speakers that "statistics show" the great number of children whose fathers have deserted their families is probably to be accounted for by the fact that day nurseries encourage family desertion. Julia Lathrop, armed with statistical information from a recent study of day nurseries, said that the study appeared to show that the great majority of children in day nurseries belonged to widowed mothers, and she blandly inquired whether the conference would therefore consider the nurseries responsible for widows. Yet everyone there knew that this was said not to be witty nor much less to confound the previous speaker, but to warn them all as to the danger of the unconsidered use of statistical data.

Julia Lathrop was long active in the Chicago Woman's Club, which she greatly admired for its civic spirit. I frequently heard her speak there, but the appeal for the moral energy of women on behalf of children which remains most vividly in my mind is an address she gave before the Annual Meeting of the National Federation of Women's Clubs at Hot Springs, Arkansas, in the early days of the War. We met then unexpectedly; I was speaking under the auspices of the Food Administration and Julia Lathrop was securing the sympathetic participation of the large number of women represented in the Federation in the work of the Children's Bureau, for she had learned to explore women's organizations for that moral enthusiasm which she constantly needed to back her official undertakings. I never heard her speak more ably than on that occasion. Certainly she accomplished what a leading newspaper described in these words:

> Her mission in life is to direct the warm-heartedness and charitable impulses of thousands of women who devote part of their time to social service through church and other organizations, into the most useful channels. Her surveys providing the scientific projects in this field are made known throughout the country as a pattern and inspiration to other groups. She is an evangel of the new charity which assumes that the American people wish to foster by every reasonable means an equality of opportunity among all children.

As always she urged her hearers to careful preparation of the task in hand. Dr. Adolf Meyer once said of her: "She is in no sense a propagandist but she is always determined to stand for getting the facts and to limit the application to the place where solid work can be done."

She did not wish women's organizations to become too respectful of even their finest traditions. She warned them against it, much as William Penn had warned his colonists not to live too much upon the traditions of their founders, "thereby encompassing yourselves with the sparks of your own fire."

Her understanding was extended to women in all situations for she never forgot Kant's maxim that human beings must be regarded as ends in themselves. She once sensed my distress at Hull-House when I was listening to a tale of woe which was rapidly rising into sheer hysteria. As she passed through the room she leaned toward me and said:

"Never mind, J.A. She is enjoying herself; some people like strong emotion as they like strong tea."

I recall her understanding of two women who were involved in the case of a dependent child for whose well being Julia Lathrop long held herself responsible.

The dependent child was a little girl of twelve who for five years had been a legally adopted child of a woman who was the harassed and overworked proprietor of a small hotel. The foster mother knew nothing concerning the care of children and in the back of her mind was the life of a "bound girl" she had known in her far-off youth. Her conscience was therefore quite clear when she required her adopted child to take care of the furnace, to tend the horse, and to wash mountainous stacks of heavy dishes far into the night. A transient guest at the hotel who was a kind hearted and well meaning woman although she was earning her living through prostitution, induced the little girl to "run away" with her into another county. The efforts of the legal guardian to reclaim her ward finally brought the case into court before the probate judge of the latter county, who conducted it without publicity in his chambers and asked Julia Lathrop to sit in on the hearing. The child of course could not be left with her newly found friend and the judge ruled that her foster mother had forfeited her right because a doctor had pronounced the child neglected and dangerously anemic. It was also an open question as to which county should pay for her if she were sent to an industrial school for dependents. The perplexed judge naturally turned to Julia Lathrop and suggested that she become the legal custodian of the child, and this was promptly arranged.

When the little girl was admitted into the Judge's chambers and told of the decision, she at once went over to Julia Lathrop's side and confidingly took her hand. Thus linked they left the courthouse together. "Are you going to be my mother now?" asked the little girl as they descended the steps. "No," said Julia Lathrop, "You have had enough mothers. The judge said, didn't he, that the State of Illinois was going to take care of you now. The Governor has asked me to do such things for the state." The little girl nodded her head in contented acquiescence but pushed her inquiries still further. "The State of Illinois has lots of towns in it, hasn't it, so that I won't ever need to go back to that one where I stayed before?" "Never so long as you live!" was the firm reply.

Of the two women involved in the case of this dependent child, Julia Lathrop said that it was baffling to find the villains so full of good intentions. The foster mother did not mean to crush the child with overwork. She was exhausted by hard work herself and considered it the duty of a virtuous family that they all should work as hard as they possibly could. The prostitute who kept the child with her for three days had carefully guarded her from any knowledge or suspicion of the unsavory character of the house in which they lodged. "How simplified life would be if we could judge people by what they think of themselves!" remarked Julia Lathrop as she considered this episode.

Both of these women felt horribly misjudged; the foster mother because she was suspected of cruelty and the prostitute because the judge intimated that she might have been a procuress while she was "merely trying to be good to an abused child whose spine was growing crooked from lifting great shovelfuls of coal too heavy for her." Neither of these women was fined or even threatened with prison; they were each let off with only a reprimand from the bench but each felt grossly misunderstood. "Self deception is one of the meanest tricks Fate plays upon us," was Julia Lathrop's sage comment as she concluded her analysis.

The little girl who was then a dependent child has long since grown up, is happily married and lives in a charming house with her children about her. To pronounce the name of Julia Lathrop in her presence brings a look into her eyes of such filial devotion and of such memories of loving kindness that to one who has ever seen this evocation, it remains a rare demonstration that the bodily shell can actually reveal that inner spirit which it seems so often merely to caricature.

Any record of her relation to women's organizations would be incomplete without something of her many pleas for the protection of children from premature and exhausting labor. The accompanying extract from one of her addresses before a Child Welfare Conference is a fine example of her use of the historic background, and of the large demands she laid upon women:

> In the great Brussels Museum, the visitor may chance upon a strange exhibit—a few groups of bones and a few rude tools lying

on the stony floor of a little cave, all carefully preserved in a big glass case. One is told that some years ago in the course of an excavation an inner rock chamber was found where undisturbed lay the skeletons of a man, a boy and a dog with the tools beside them, just as they are now shown in the museum. The students' interpretation is that long ages ago the man and the boy were working to enlarge their dwelling place and as they toiled a slide closed the mouth of the cave and they were left to perish, the dog with them, "man's only friend on this chance planet," as the Belgian poet says. On the ever-ready picture postcard the scene is described as the first industrial accident, but it might also be described with equal probability as our earliest record of child labor.

This much is clear—the cave man was at work striving to secure a better place to live in—a primitive and unceasing human activity. He died in the attempt, as untold members have died since. Whether the helper was son or slave or both in one, we do not know, but he was working at the same task with the man and met the same end. To trace the extent to which the child must share the hazards of the struggle for a better standard of life, the age at which in different stages of human development he must put off childish things would be to trace the progress of man toward civilization. We know that it was untold thousands of years after the cave man before the father ceased to have the power of life and death over his child, and we know too well that the ideal of social justice which recognizes the right of every child to education and opportunity is far from realized in any country to this day. Through the long reaches of race history, changes in the status of the child came slowly and late; suddenly in a few recent generations unparalleled advances have been made in the protection of the child from untimely labor and from the necessity of self-support. These advances have come chiefly because the discoveries of science have made possible free general interchange of thought with the resulting mental and moral stimulus. Also these discoveries have already made physically possible universal comfort and refinement of life though we are not yet skilled enough to insure equitably those living conditions which may afford the children of every family a fair start in life. Our laws and actions lag behind the attainments science already has made possible. What is now almost common knowledge of the laws of health and sanitation fills volumes—what we neglect to do in obedience to these laws would fill larger volumes.

The address continued: "All we can do to save our faces with posterity is to go on experimentally in the slowly increasing knowledge of our day, doing what the cave man did—trying to improve things."

Another of her speeches concludes: "There is no dividing line between so-called economic legislation and welfare work. Everything which affects the life of the nation—be it agricultural relief, taxation, labor, or railroad legislation—affects the lives of children and the welfare of citizens. It is all, in a way, welfare legislation, and conversely there is no such thing as pure welfare legislation which is all fundamentally economic."

A Washington correspondent once said of Julia Lathrop,—"I hardly ever agree with anything she says, but I would walk twenty miles to hear her speak." Another added, "Her willingness to speak was based upon her devotion to the cause she served—first and foremost in her heart was the cause of the Nation's children, and after them the whole body of the poor, the unfortunate, the criminals, the 'submerged tenth.'"

The Illinois Immigrants' Protective League of which Julia Lathrop was a founder and devoted trustee, was formally organized in 1908 although for years previously a group of public spirited women had received from the immigration authorities at Ellis Island the lists of unaccompanied girls whose destination was Chicago. Some of these young women who were coming to meet their families were in actual danger of being decoyed on the train journey between New York and Chicago by the men in the so-called white slave trade, who found it cheaper to utilize the girls already here than to transport others. Such services for the young immigrants led to many others, and the League not only befriended newcomers by locating relatives and helping in the first adjustments but constantly enlarged its activities.

The Immigrants' Protective League had performed such services for more than ten years when, largely because of the efforts of Julia Lathrop and other members of the Board of Directors, the Illinois Legislature finally established a commission which assumed state responsibility for the assimilation of foreign born groups residing in Illinois. The Immigration Commission was appointed by Governor Lowden in 1919 and for the next two years the work of the Immigrants' Protective League was merged with the Commission and thereby made state wide. Grace Abbott, then the Secretary of the League, was made the executive officer of the State Commission and served in that capacity until the appropriation for the State Commission was vetoed by Governor Lowden's successor. The League again became a voluntary social agency and resumed its former activities.

At the time of its reorganization, the League established its offices in one of the Hull-House buildings and has remained there ever since. Mrs. Kenneth Rich, a Hull-House resident, has become its able secretary. Between her and Julia Lathrop there long existed an understanding friendship fostered not only through their mutual interests in the problems brought before the League but through many other public spirited undertakings. In this protection of the immigrants, Julia Lathrop was also closely associated with another resident of Hull-House, Mrs. Alfred Kohn, with whom she went one spring into eastern Europe to learn at first hand of the difficulties attending migration from one part of the world to another after the War. They interviewed various groups, who, unable to secure passports from their own countries, found themselves marooned in hostile countries from which it was almost impossible to escape legally. With Mrs. Kohn, Julia Lathrop attended a meeting of the International Migration Service in Geneva. They found the same problems discussed there which as members of the Immigrants' Protective League they had so often encountered in Chicago. Perhaps Mrs. Kohn better than any other of Julia Lathrop's friends knew of her deep concern for the difficulties surrounding immigrants in Europe and of the complications awaiting them on their arrival at Ellis Island.

Before she went to Washington and after her return Julia Lathrop was not only active as a Board member of the Immigrants' Protective League in suggesting policies for the organization, in formulating its public statements and fostering its international relations, but she was constantly concerned with the concrete cases which she referred directly to the League, and always "followed up" to find out what had become of those people who regarded her as an intimate friend.

Out of many letters from her on file in the office is one of May, 1928, which describes the need of a young Japanese student at Rockford College for the kind of advice and help which Miss Lathrop knew so well how to enlist.

Her letter states:

In Rockford there is now residing with his wife a man by the name of J.T.H., an artist and furniture decorator. He came into the country before the Act of 1924 and can, I understand, remain here indefinitely. His wife came two years ago as a student. Their history is about as follows, as far as it regards their present plight:

Mrs. H. has the degree of B.A. from the Japan Women's University, Tokio, the largest women's university in Japan. It is an endowed institution of high standing. Six years ago she became engaged to Mr. H. and though this seems to have little to do with the case, he came over here, earned the money and paid her tuition for four years because as he said to me he wished her to have an education. When she arrived at Seattle she was able to enter as a student, came to Chicago and was married to Mr. H. who was then working for the Pullman Company as a draughtsman and at the same time taking a course in interior decorating. Mrs. H. took an English course in the immigrants' (public) school and Saturday morning, studied in the Academy of Art. In 1926 both came to Rockford and have been here until the present time, Mr. H. doing furniture decorating in a factory and working on private orders and Mrs. H. studying at Rockford College.

She can remain in the United States as a student until 1930 only, according to their understanding of the law. They seem to have discovered that an editor or journalist or importer or exporter and those engaged perhaps in some other professional occupations can remain in this country indefinitely. Mr. and Mrs. H. both think that she can get a position as corresponding journalist for some Japanese paper. She has written somewhat for publication in school journals and the like, and seems to have an intelligent idea of the things Japanese women would like to know about the United States—child welfare and fashions are subjects of very great interest over there, she says.

As you will see from this preamble, the question now is whether she can be allowed to change her status and remain here, supposing that she can show a bona fide position as a journalist. Also what other alternative to returning to Japan is open to them? I do not know that I have made the matter very clear. If not let me try again. It appears that the inspectors are watchful to make sure that she goes to school in good faith. As I suspect has happened before, they have in one instance at least received an intimation that a lawyer for $300 could "make it all right," and I think they lack the $300, and also are unwilling to risk any such negotiation. They are very anxious about the whole matter and very uncertain as to how to proceed. I told them that I was connected with the society in Chicago whose business it was to help people honestly and disinterestedly under such circumstances; and that at least they could rely implicitly on whatever information they received. I shall be grateful for your help. These are honorable, refined, intelligent persons, but they know the law is the thing!

A brief was assembled for Julia Lathrop's perusal, which her keen mind was quick to appreciate. It set forth an array of regulations and provisions surrounding the position of this young woman in the United States: (1) The specifications of the Naturalization Laws regarding ineligibility to citizenship; (2) the sections of the Immigration Act of 1924 relating to admission of "ineligibles," of temporary visitors, and of "non-quota students"; (3) the Administrative Rules pertaining thereto; (4) the inability of persons in the United States, under this Act, to change from one immigration status to another, even though the status had changed in fact; (5) the provisions of the Immigration Act of 1917 regarding entry into the United States of persons from the "Barred Zone"; (6) the 1907 "Gentlemen's Agreement" with Japan; (7) the 1911 Treaty of Commerce and Navigation with Japan; (8) Federal Court decisions relating to Japanese in the United States.

Within these statutory walls, however, Julia Lathrop saw the natural desire of a young husband and wife to remain together; the contribution he was making to America, the advantage of post-graduate work in this country in preparation for the wife's profession back in her homeland, and the wider implications of international understanding and good will.

When the wife's temporary immigration permit neared its date of expiration, and in response to the young woman's application for an extension in order that her studies might be completed, the Department of Labor had advised her that it would be denied, Julia Lathrop again came to her assistance.

Because she knew, partly through her own previous connection with the United States Department of Labor, that high public officials are often "set upon" for personal favors, she always guarded scrupulously against any undue impositions upon persons in authority. She saw human need, however, above human rules and regulations. In this instance, therefore, she wrote immediately to the administrative official charged with review of immigration affairs at Washington—then the Second Assistant Secretary of Labor W. W. Husband—setting the facts plainly before him, and appealing on the basis of their merit in behalf of the husband and wife in Illinois. Her plea was successful. The United States Department of Labor granted an extension for continued study. Then a graduate scholarship was offered by the University of Chicago where Mrs. H. secured the degree of Master of Science in Home Economics in the summer of 1933.

In such cases, as well as in matters of public policy Julia Lathrop never failed to prove her unfailing sense of justice.

She was much interested in the efforts of the Immigrants' Protective League to modify Federal legislation: She heartily approved the League's opposition to proposals for the registration of aliens believing it to be un-American, impossible to enforce and a serious bar to the forming of good citizenship in the United States. She also worked with the League for the removal of naturalization obstacles and for the mitigation of the hardship of separated families. These hardships were stressed by a group of social workers in a petition to Congress that if no other way could be found to unite these broken families the quota regulation be legally suspended in regard to those who had become separated during the war. They stated that about 173,000 so-called "fireside relatives," including husbands, wives, parents and children were then living in other countries but dependent upon relatives living here since no provision in the quota system had been made for such cases.

Julia Lathrop was much distressed as we all were when the earliest outbreaks of gang violence in Chicago, more or less typical of those throughout the country, became associated with immigrants. We were convinced however that the gangsters were bootlegging, racketeering, conducting gambling houses, or systematically stealing automobiles only because they had been able to secure the connivance and, in certain towns, the participation of the police themselves. Their successful methods of corruption often involved far-reaching political and business affiliations. It was commonly said in this later period that the police were not so much concerned to protect the community as to

protect themselves from exposure, and that the criminals had the police "on the run," using an expressive phrase from the Irish revolution.
It was obvious that certain men in protected areas under a corrupt city
administration were given vice privileges in the way of running ques-
tionable dance halls or were immune from arrest although conducting a "fence" for automobiles or other stolen property.

It was much easier to blame the immigrants for the increase of
crime resulting from such a situation than it was to make a determined
effort to clean up the ramified political corruption. But the resulting
public impression of the immigrant is often very disastrous, especially
in times of economic distress when the last comer into the competi-
tion for employment is so easily regarded as an intruder.

Julia Lathrop was therefore much pleased when the National Commission of Law Observance and Enforcement appointed by President
Hoover, issued Report 10 on Crime and the Foreign Born in June, 1931.
The report, signed by the Chairman, George W. Wickersham and the
other members of the Commission, stated that in proportion to their
respective numbers, the foreign born commit considerably fewer crimes
than the native born; that the foreign born approach the record of the
native born most closely in the commission of crimes involving personal violence, and that in crimes for gain the native born greatly exceed the foreign born. The General Conclusions of the report, written
by Dr. Edith Abbott, states:

> For more than a century there has been continuously in this
> country a clamorous group who have tended to emphasize only
> the difficulties connected with immigration and to lose sight of all
> its benefits and effects. . . .
> Charging our high crime rates against the foreign born is merely
> evading the real difficulties of life instead of trying to solve them,
> to continue to follow the method of adopting one policy because
> it is the "easy way"—the line of least resistance—and rejecting an-
> other method because it is more difficult. But an attempt to face
> squarely the more difficult problems of life is more in line with our
> American traditions.

When she had resigned from the Children's Bureau President
Coolidge appointed Julia Lathrop a member of a Federal Commission

to look into the conditions on Ellis Island. Julia Lathrop encountered there once more well meaning officials who had so fallen into routine and preconceived conception of their duty that in many instances they were quite incapable of seeing individual cases. For instance, the women and children were allowed to go out of doors only one hour a day although the sea might be ever so blue and sparkling in the sunshine. The reason given for this restriction was that they could furnish guards only for a short time each day, and when the Committee inquired why guards were required for women and children the reply was that a young man who was unattended had once been able to swim ashore and there was no telling what might happen. This excessive care was also extended to the Italians from the orange groves of southern Italy who were not allowed to have oranges "because they were so ignorant that they would eat the skins." When Julia Lathrop told me this story I remarked that Italians probably knew how not to eat orange skins before Columbus discovered America, to which she replied, with a delicious Irish twist to her words, "Sure but they weren't furriners thin."

12

Journey around the World, 1910–1911

🙥 In 1910 and 1911 Julia and her widowed sister, Anna Lathrop Case, went around the world together. Their "Aunt Matt," a missionary from whom on her visits to Rockford they had heard stories of India all their lives, had finally retired and with her friend Miss Ward had settled in California in 1910, and she urged the journey on her nieces. She wanted them to see her beloved India and particularly the mission at Allahabad, of which she had been the head for many years. "Aunt Matt," more formally Miss Martha Lathrop, and Miss Grace Ward had been sent out to India together by the Women's Union Mission Board at a time when the condition of child-widows in India, with "suttee" still unprohibited after more than a hundred years of English government, had greatly stirred the hearts of women throughout Christendom. The two young women were at first together at Calcutta, then separated when Miss Ward shrewdly bought a large place at Cawnpore as a strategic spot for directing missionary efforts, and then finally were reunited to spend many years together at the mission in the fascinating city of Allahabad.

Martha Lathrop and Grace Ward were visitors at Hull-House when they returned from their mission in India. We were a little afraid of them at first, for as a group we were not very orthodox, but they quickly reassured us because our method of approach to the neighborhood seemed to them so like that employed by foreign missionaries, such as our efforts to learn a foreign language—a little broken polyglot, we used to say, was what we really needed—our friendship with the day nursery mothers and with the children in the kindergarten, our efforts to help the young people who were ambitious "for an education." When

we insisted that our activities were not as missionary activities tradi-
tionally had been, mere lures to something else, but that we were "serving God for naught," the dear old ladies replied that so did the missionaries and pointed to hospitals and schools throughout the Orient.

I vividly recall one incident during their visit: Julia Lathrop who had
long disappointed her aunt by failure to openly profess adherence to a
set creed, was much entertained to find that through observing our daily
activities at Hull-House her aunt had concluded that the unbeliever had
been thoroughly snared at last by the net of conventional good works.
Discerning this, Julia was much touched and said to me one evening,
"The dear angel is so pleased by this sign of grace that she has mo-
mentarily forgotten her own doctrine of 'by faith alone'. I quite dread
the moment when she shall remember it, for all her innocent pleasure
may then vanish." She added: "Aunt Matt is so good all through—she
hasn't one trace of the attitude manifested by the English clergy toward
Elizabeth Frye. I was reading last night about her amazing prison reforms and of that wag among the preachers who said: 'Mrs. Frye is very
unpopular with the clergy because her example of living active virtue
disturbs our repose and gives birth to distressing comparisons,' and he
added as a supreme jest, 'we long to burn her alive.' Aunt Matt would
never have said that, even if she were trying to be funny as hard as the
English clergyman was, for she couldn't imagine such a state of mind."

It was late in the evening when she said this, and we were standing
by the long Hull-House stairway at the head of which Aunt Matt's
black skirt had just disappeared. I spoke impulsively, for I knew Julia's
dislike of haphazard assumptions: "That phrase 'good all through' exactly suits you, J. Lathrop! Perhaps a flair for righteous conduct is a
family strain which comes out in one generation after another as a fa-
cility for music does in other families." She looked at me in blank astonishment and replied, in a comic imitation of the university lecturer:
"Don't generalize on insufficient data, J.A. It is a great temptation but
in this case fully one-half of your data is absolutely off. Fifty per cent
of inaccuracy is a very large margin."

Julia Lathrop and Mrs. Case stayed for some weeks in the very
house in which their aunt had lived for so many years. It was built in
the old fashion of houses in India for the English, with very large high
rooms and it stood in a large compound.

Many of Julia Lathrop's experiences in India and my own a decade later when my friend Mary Smith and I made the same journey, were connected with visitors at Hull-House. In the very early days we heard the stirring talk by Pundita Ramabai who had set herself against the treatment of child widows and had established schools for their rescue; she was followed by Sister Nivedita, a delightful Englishwoman converted to an Eastern cult who gave us what we perhaps much needed, an inside interpretation of many customs which had degenerated with the passage of time.

☙

Julia Lathrop and her sister, Mrs. Case, sailed from New York in the early winter of 1910. After a visit in Egypt they took a P & O steamer through the Red Sea to Ceylon, landing in Colombo in December. They spent Christmas in the old buried city of Anurbhapura, which as the ancient capital of Ceylon had ranked with Nineveh and Babylon in its colossal proportions. Each of its four walls, so recently rescued from the jungle, is sixteen miles long as if fitted to the huge tropical growth which spreads about it in every direction.

The lovely island of Ceylon holds many treasures of beauty in its jungles and mountains. Its educational affairs which the British administered quite independently of India, showed the enthusiastic attention which had been given to them by various well known English educators living there. Julia Lathrop and her sister during their visit in Kandy, saw something of the fine work carried on in Trinity College by Alexander Fraser and when I reached Ceylon a decade later some of the students whom she had known had become important factors in the Social Service League of Ceylon formally organized two years after her visit.

This League, like organizations with similar names in India, occupied a position mid-way between politics and philanthropy. The most notable of those organizations, called the Servants of India Society, with flourishing branches in various cities, Julia Lathrop first encountered in Bombay, as I did later. This society, founded in 1905, is a distinguished group vowed to poverty and lifelong service. It is an interesting combination of Eastern asceticism and renunciation of worldly ambition combined with western standards of social reform and scientific methods. Apparently the devoted young men wished to make clear to the common people of India that a return to native government does not necessarily consist of maharajahs riding about on painted elephants. The home rule they advocated would continue the beneficence embodied in public hospitals, educational institutions and irrigation systems established by the British. They also wished to make clear that the British were not responsible for all modern improvements in India or elsewhere. That railroads, for instance, were the common achievement of advancing civilization, and need not be considered as the gift of an alien government. The Servants of India Society were in no sense adherents to the doctrine of non-violence. Gandhi in 1912 was still in South Africa working out his strategy of non-resistance, but there were many evidences in the growing Nationalist Movement of its later development.

When I visited Bombay ten years later, the Servants of India were convening the fourth session of the All India Social Workers Conference which issued a fine program of practical work and study, urging among other things that "Universities in India should provide in the curricula of arts degree for optional courses in the social study with a view to afford opportunities of theoretical study to social workers." This program was urged only four years after the Chicago School of Civics and Philanthropy, with whose beginning Julia Lathrop had been so closely identified, had been taken over by the University of Chicago.

At the date of my visit in 1923 a university settlement had been started by one of the Servants of India, a Hindu graduate of the New York School of Philanthropy, who had also lived at Toynbee Hall in London.

The Society had a representative in the Legislative Council, established by the British as a first test, as it were, of self-government in India and anticipating a dominion status. Its representative, Mr. Joshi, was intelligently fostering a program of remedial legislation; attendance at one of its sessions was reminiscent, in its subjects of discussion at least, of the British Parliament itself. Mr. Joshi was later a delegate from the Legislative Council to the Labor Conference called by President Wilson in Washington in 1919 under the auspices of the International Labor Office. It was the first labor conference on American soil to discuss its problems with the sanction and participation of Governments as well as employers. Mr. Joshi's eloquent speeches added greatly to its effectiveness.

Years afterwards at a Child Welfare Conference, Julia Lathrop said:

> No one who heard the discussions on child labor in the International Child Labor Congress in Washington in 1919 will ever forget the vigor and steadiness of the Oriental members who urged the recognition of the right of the Indian, Chinese and Japanese children to lengthened years of education and shortened years of toil. The whole world is at one in its sense of the public importance of child protection, but it is only too clear that social and economic questions, national and international, must be solved before all children have their rights.
>
> The theory of child labor restriction is a doctrine which leads far. It applies to every child of every race. It tolerates no exceptions or exemptions from the duty of the elder generation to provide for every child an education which shall develop his powers and give him a fair chance in the world of tomorrow. The International Labor Bureau of the League of Nations already deeply engaged in worldwide study of child labor must stir the imagination and the conscience of every democratic thinker who tries to measure its future power of aiding in the emancipation of childhood.

With the recession of events into the past, with all the readjustments of values which the mere passage of time brings, it is curious how a small incident sometimes remains in one's memory as charged with special significance. At the moment of Julia Lathrop's journey those of us at Hull-House who were members of the Association for Labor Legislation had been much interested in the world wide effort to establish international control over the use of a dangerous form of phosphorus in the manufacture of matches which produced the so-called phossy jaw, a very painful and disfiguring disease, sometimes even fatal if the exposure were continued. It was obvious that if one nation forbade the use of this white phosphorus and ordered a substitute which was more expensive the manufacturers of that land would be at a disadvantage in the world market. An international convention in Berne in 1906 had dealt with the matter and all the industrial nations of Europe had agreed to discontinue the use of poisonous phosphorus, an agreement into which the United States was prevented from

entering by the Constitution. It was not until 1912, the year after Julia
Lathrop returned from her journey, that the American regulation was
finally obtained through the Interstate Commerce Act which forbade
the shipping of the old type of matches from one state to another. So
that when she was in the Orient the United States and China were the
only match-producing countries still using white phosphorus. The
question was naturally discussed by people whom Julia Lathrop met
throughout her journey in that year when there was much talk of the
entrance of Oriental countries with their low labor standards into com-
petition with the western world. This situation was almost a forecast
of the later attitude on the part of the United States toward the League
of Nations, concerning which I was so often challenged during my
journey in the Orient in 1923.

It was inevitable that Julia Lathrop should have been much distressed by what she saw of Oriental poverty. The conditions in southern India, especially in the neighborhood of Madras, were almost incredible. In addition to the starving agriculturists there are in India
38,000,000 landless workers and servants who continually engage in a
bitter struggle for existence and at the very bottom rung of the economic ladder are 60,000,000 outcasts, so-called untouchables, landless, penniless and destitute. One's days are darkened by foreboding
and the nights are sleepless when the situation in southern India really grips the traveler. I recall the return from India of Canon Barnett,
the first warden of Toynbee Hall, who with his wife visited at Hull-
House on their way to England. He found it almost impossible to speak
of the daily suffering and starvation, although he had long been familiar with the bitter poverty of East London.

Almost as interesting as the social service activities were the manifestations of the women's movement already astir in India. In Calcutta
the travelers encountered a women's organization with a Dowager Ma-
harani as President which that very year had reorganized on a national
basis. It forecast even then an organization now in Bombay which unites
Hindu, Parsee and Moslem women in philanthropic work—"a union
of India's daughters for the purpose of India's welfare."

Julia Lathrop, although prepared by her knowledge of this early organization of Eastern women, found it hard to believe the report I carried to her a decade later from my visit in Bombay, that not only were

the women voting at municipal elections but that one Hindu woman, Sarojini Naidu, had been elected a member of the city council. Mrs. Naidu a few years later visited us several times at Hull-House during her lecture tour in the United States. Although she was a friend of Gandhi and had been his Vice-President in the Indian National Congress, the red-letter occasions to me were the times we induced her to read aloud to us after dinner from her books of exquisite lyrics which Edmund Gosse first cherished when they were but fugitive pieces.

In Calcutta they saw something of the Brahmo Samaj to which we had been so charmingly introduced by the Hindu scholar Mozumdar, who came very often to Hull-House during the Congress of Religions held in connection with the World's Fair in Chicago in 1893. The women in this religious group living in Calcutta had enjoyed the unrestricted freedom of western women for three generations and many of them had been educated in England and other parts of the world. The Brahmo Samaj group reflected the rationalistic point of view which Unitarianism seems to exhibit everywhere, although this particular society declared that it endeavored "more to stimulate honest thinking and to promote fearless action than to spread any particular creed." Julia Lathrop became much interested in these pioneer college women and in their plans for public service.

The traveler in India interested in the woman's movement becomes conscious of the remnants of matriarchates on the edge of India, and even incorporated within its territory. It is quite disconcerting to be introduced to a bright-eyed student who tells you that she is reading economics and government with university professors because the women in her province hold such responsible governmental positions. The veiled Mohammedan women, carried to the polls in curtained litters that they may cast their votes, are no more surprising. To suffragists the woman's situation in the East is a matter of unending interest.

The travelers, Julia Lathrop and Mrs. Case, finally arrived in the city of Allahabad, which must have seemed to them like the peace of Journey's End. The city is at the confluence of the Ganges and the Jinura rivers joined I believe by a secret river flowing beneath the huge fort which Akbar built. Because of these sacred streams Allahabad has become one of the most noted centers in India for pilgrimages. An annual fair is held at the great bathing festival in the full moon of the Hindu month Magh, lasting for thirty days and attracting thousands of pilgrims. But every twelfth year there is a special Kumbh-Mela attended by a million devotees. Julia Lathrop and Mrs. Case were in Allahabad at the time of this great pilgrimage and added one more vivid impression to those always associated with India, of a myriad population too vast to be numbered, and an unforgettable memory of the affectionate worship everywhere paid to Mother Ganges. This impression of pious pilgrims was happily quite unlike the dramatic scene the traveler retains of the Ganges if he sees it only at Benares with the banks covered with smoking funeral pyres—those of the poor so inadequate as to fuel that not only the ashes of the dead are thrown into the river but unconsumed limbs as well. Mother Ganges, however, with her powerful undercurrent of glacial water, bears them impartially onward to the sea.

At Calcutta the travelers took a boat to Rangoon, then a river craft upon the Irrawaddy with its charm and glamour, to Mandalay.

With all its poesy the one lasting impression of Burma is astonishment over the activity of the women who carry on about half the trade of the country and show remarkable aptitude for it as well as for banking and other purely financial activities. It does not in the end seem illogical, although still amazing, that Burmese women should have had the pioneer vote among eastern women and now hold the franchise on the same terms as English women.

The travelers took a boat from Singapore to Hongkong, from whence they went to Manila. In the Philippine Islands, Julia Lathrop was much interested in the condition surrounding the children and their response to the new educational opportunities. It was said to be her penetrating report on the public schools of the Philippines which had come into President Taft's hands, that greatly assisted her appointment to the Children's Bureau the next year. Judge Taft, who had been the first Governor-General of the Philippine Islands after they were taken over by the United States, was of course enormously interested in the development of the public school system which had been established there.

When Mary Smith and I were in Manila, Madame Jaime C. de Veyra, whose husband had represented the Philippine Islands—in that curious fashion in which dependencies are represented in Congress—had been a friend of Julia Lathrop's in Washington and was most understanding of what the Bureau was trying to do with the Philippine children. The leading woman's club in Manila was enthusiastically following out the Bureau's direction for the establishment of child welfare stations not only in Manila but hoping to include the remoter islands as well.

And so the journey proceeded. At one point, as if to round out the impression of Oriental women, it afforded a glimpse of a woman as Royalty. In Tokio a Vassar classmate of Mrs. Case who was head of a Presbyterian mission, put them up in a room with a beautiful view of the mountain and the first day at breakfast told them that the Japanese Crown Prince and his wife were about to start for King Edward's funeral. Through Miss West's special ticket to the station platform they saw the Royal couple walking up and down and bowing to everyone. The little Princess going so gently, was very conscious of everything that was happening. She was said to be wearing the European clothes purchased when she went to the King's coronation, she certainly wore a European gown with a train as well as a big hat.

The travelers stopped for one day only at Honolulu and arrived in California to be met by the two returned missionaries who had been so eager to send them out and were anxious to hear how their beloved India was faring.

It is surprising how well Julia Lathrop understood those earlier missionary efforts; she who especially disliked "those zealots of every class and race who demand immediate acquiescence in their own opinions while looking upon the ideas that fail to correspond with their own as rank heresy or even as a mark of rascality." It was characteristic of her to approach such a situation with consideration and with tolerance, not only with good will but with understanding. Her spiritual trustworthiness never failed although she knew how easily our dark and confused human affairs may become further complicated by error and illusion.

She had long since learned to look with indulgence upon human perplexity and upon its very unwillingness to understand. She once said that she loved the world largely because of its "variegated manifestations."

I know of no one who returned from that marvelous journey around the world more enriched with "the spoils of time" than Julia Lathrop. She illustrated Emerson's statement that "the earth moves and the mind opens." I confess to a certain confusion of mind as to what we discussed together upon her return in 1911 and upon mine in 1923. It may be that I recall most easily in connection with her those experiences which we thus shared in retrospect. I do not mean to imply that we ever sat down to talk of "our travels." We were both much too busy and absorbed in current undertakings for that, but because I had been able to see the consummation of certain social efforts carried on with every possible handicap, of which she had known the beginning, we both gained a fresh confidence in the possibilities of social advance through concerted action. At least "the kingdom of the mind" was enlarged by the mutual consciousness.

I imagine that such a journey around the world always more or less toughens and objectifies life experience. Both of us had often seen the human spirit struggle with its own shortcomings and with the result of its own mistakes and weaknesses; but such a journey gave a view of life's limitations caused by geographic and economic conditions that so often circumscribe action and suppress aspiration. We came back with a poignant knowledge of the bitter poverty in which so large a portion of the world population lives; of the massive weight of heredity; of the despotism of those old women in complete control of eastern households who are so insistent that outworn ideas and usages must be meticulously observed; of the widespread bigotry which would bring the "divine multiplicity of human life, under one yoke."

But in spite of such serious reflection, Julia Lathrop made the experiences of her journey a bridge linking up remoter time and space with the universality of human experience, and to the end her heart held the world in friendly affection.

The journey itself added an historic background and a wider understanding to her long experience in dealing with the helpless, with the poor and with those handicapped in mind and body. It all furnished a wonderful preparation for the Children's Bureau, to which President Taft appointed her the first Chief, in 1912.

13

The Last Decade, 1922–1932

✍ After Julia Lathrop's return from Washington she and her sister Mrs. Case built for themselves a very attractive house in Rockford on the bank of the Rock River out of the actual "Milwaukee cream bricks" of which the family house had been built and made a delightful home together. In her own library, which was entered so unexpectedly from the front hall, she had collected her many books, photographs, papers and graphs into a coherent whole and here she continued to work to the end of her life. The drawing room was beautifully furnished with Oriental porcelains which she and her sister had procured during their journeys, the whole giving an impression of restraint and distinction which it is not easy to achieve.

It was during this period, after her resignation from the Children's Bureau, that we again saw Julia Lathrop more frequently at Hull-House than during her strenuous years in Washington. It must have been during the War that I recall a conversation with the residents who were still in the dining room after dinner. Dr. Alice Hamilton, who for some years had made studies in the poisonous trades for the Federal Department of Labor and was at that moment investigating the munitions industries, told of a recent experience in a smokeless powder works which she had found quite frightening. Her guide had taken her up to a room on the third story where there was an enormous bin for the reception of a stream of smokeless powder which came pouring down. The guide asked the men how the static was acting and the answer was, "Not badly." "Static," remarked the guide, "is our worst trouble. If a spark should start an explosion here, don't you wait, just jump into that chute and slide down to the ground and then start running. Don't look behind you." The startled residents laughed nervously at the tale much to Julia Lathrop's indignation. She said that such inspecting was as dangerous as being in the trenches and was no cause for even simulated mirth. She then pulled herself up and added in a reflective tone that, even from the horrible statistics of the war coming in every day, life in the trenches was not as dangerous as being a baby in certain parts of the United States. The babies at that moment, in one country after another, had a higher death rate than the soldiers at the front.

It is in connection with the investigation of munition plants during the war that Alice Hamilton writes of her:

> During the War, when my field was munition plants making high explosives and loading shells, I used always to stay with Julia Lathrop when I came to Washington to make my reports. That was a strange time in the munition industry, a time of greed masquerading as patriotism, of incompetence or indifference in places where one had a right to expect understanding and help. The men whom I was trying to protect were largely casual laborers, unskilled and unorganized, of no importance to politicians and despised by organized labor, and they worked for employers who at the time felt themselves to be and were the most powerful class in the country. Many an evening did I spend in that apartment in The Ontario pouring out my long suppressed rage against munition makers, military men and the American Federation of Labor, to Julia Lathrop's untiring and sympathetic ears, and always she brought me to a more reasonable and practical frame of mind.

I recall another talk with Julia Lathrop in the Hull-House dining room. I had returned from an educational conference and was expressing some impatience about the people who think that everything will come out all right if they only educate the children into paragons who will make over the world. I contended that these educators yield to a curious temptation to instruct posterity and are so anxious about future generations that they do nothing at all about contemporary affairs. I ended by saying: "Don't you let your precious Bureau, J. Lathrop, add to the general confusion by making people believe that they can go to war or do any other wicked thing they choose because they are saving the world by giving the young a progressive education. The Bureau itself will do more harm than good if it justifies shifting all responsibility upon the shoulders of the next generation." Her reply was unexpectedly mild for I deserved a retort which she could easily have given me. She remarked that we all knew that mankind seemed almost incapable of learning from experience which would seem the natural way to learn. The best that the Children's Bureau could do was what a young man once said of his college professor, "He did not merely increase our experience, he left us more alert for what had not yet been experienced and more hopeful about it."

I think that it was during this same conversation on the education of children that someone questioned her as to the tests the Children's Bureau had adopted to determine the average child. She replied that there was really no such creature as the average child; that the very phrase always reminded her of the old farmer down in Missouri who said that his two boys struck a splendid average because one was bow-legged and the other knock-kneed—"Together they couldn't be beat."

In connection with these trivial stories which I hope may illustrate Julia Lathrop's wit and wisdom, I should like in Quaker fashion to bear the following testimony:

Sydney Smith once said: "English gaiety is seldom come at lawfully. Friendship or propriety or principle are sacrificed to obtain it. We cannot produce it without more effort than it is worth." Sydney Smith was doubtless able to write this because he himself never made sacrifices in order to obtain gaiety. A friend once said to him: "You have been laughing at me for the last seven years and you never said anything which I wished unsaid." Through half a century of friendship with Julia Lathrop I can multiply the seven years by seven more years and make the same assertion in regard to her. She combined the small virtues with the great ones and refuted Sydney Smith's own statement that "The order of human excellence is so often inverted that great talents are considered as an excuse for the absence of obscure virtues."

After her retirement from the Children's Bureau in 1922 she became president of the Illinois League of Women Voters and during her term she was often in Chicago, sometimes to deliver one of her stirring addresses. She shared the widespread enthusiasm of women in securing the vote, and wrote of it:

Future historians are likely to hold that the most surprising and prophetic event in our War period was the quiet, worldwide enfranchisement of uncounted millions of women in countries differing as much in race, governments and traditions as Mexico, Canada, the United States, Lithuania, Czechoslovakia and India. This enfranchisement creates a new world feeling among women, a new world power of unknown strength. It can mark the beginning of a new world peace if we work hard enough for just world politics.

Will women take their new rights with seriousness? Have they indeed an unselfish solidarity of interest in social progress? And if they have, are they willing to do the dull work, to carry on the painstaking unprejudiced studies which have become imperatively necessary to effective political progress?

She was always a little apprehensive however in the early days that women throughout the country would be so pleased with securing the vote that they would tend to consider that, in itself, a sufficient achievement. So she warned: "A woman voter must remember that politics and political action are only the mill and not the grist, a means and not an end." She pointed out the inevitable temptation to slacken the pace, for "it is not in human nature that any persons who possess power can be as active as those who are pursuing it." She assured women that they were engaged in a revolution, for, she said, "it is nothing less than a revolution that women have emerged from their kitchens to ask searching questions about the why and wherefore of the costs they and their husbands have ages-long accepted with fatalistic discontent."

Mrs. Kenneth Rich of Hull-House, who served as vice-president two years when Julia Lathrop was president for the State of Illinois of the League of Women Voters, has said of her League activities:

But the pictures of Miss Lathrop that especially come flooding to mind are those during her presidency of the Illinois League of Women Voters, from 1922 to 1924, and her later service as vice-president and counsellor in public welfare of the National League of Women Voters.

One saw her at citizenship schools at the University of Chicago, at Northwestern University, at Loyola, or setting forth to address the young women in the schools and small colleges scattered over Illinois. She spoke of the League as "an emergency self-educational order," and a "laboratory method in political education." When work demanded study she led the way into principles and technique and structure of government, federal aid, amendment of the constitution of the United States, the Gateway Amendment in Illinois. She had practiced "efficiency in Government."

One saw her at the State capitol when the first woman legislator Mrs. Lottie Holman O'Neill was seated in the Illinois General Assembly, captivating the members of the legislature with her statement of the hopes and purposes of women in politics. Or she would be seen at Springfield when the League's legislative measures were under fire, appearing at committee hearings or explaining to members of the legislature personally matters of child labor, the protection of maternity and infancy, the shorter work day and the minimum wage, the woman's farm colony, women on juries, women in political parties, the educational measures.

These questions, she once told a state gathering, "touch the family life and happiness at every point and they require joint action by law and administration to preserve the dignity and health and decent standards of the family. The League has not taken four years to learn that Aristotle spoke as would a good citizen of Illinois when he refused to consider separately the family and politics and ethics." Or she would modestly enter the outside battle camps of those measures—the medical societies opposing co-operation in the Sheppard-Towner act, manufacturers' groups still clinging to the legal right to employ child labor. Miss Lathrop may have winced at some affronts but she did not withdraw the efforts to protect childhood. These efforts were always remote from any consideration of personal comfort or personal gain.

And when public recognition came to another woman of Illinois, the judge of the Juvenile Court in whose election Miss Lathrop was deeply concerned, she was there at the induction of Miss Mary Bartelme in 1923. "It is an honor too generously bestowed, I fear, that I," she said, "who am no Portia, should be asked to speak in a court room on this occasion. . . . We rejoice because her election gives to those who are the young clients of this court . . . the full benefit of her generous wisdom. . . . Students of law and society . . . are encouraged by the growing efforts to make law serve social order by more inspiring and reassuring structures than our prisons." She believed in women in government, from precinct to capitol, but in the merit system for them as for all. "Women," she said, "cannot afford to be incompetent." She herself had led the way—the first woman to hold high public office in this country. But she said nothing of that.

Or one would see her taking the train to speak to a newly organized local League of Women Voters out in the state, on the meaning, of this training for citizenship, at Saline perhaps, or Galesburg, or De Kalb, or Morris, or Jacksonville or some more distant point. These speeches meant red letter days for fledgling Leagues. She told them of their "personal interest and concern"; counseled them to "catch step with men"; urged "the voter to stop, look and listen, and not to vote on the run without knowing what or why."

At state conventions women crowded to business sessions because she was presiding. She was the ornament of a banquet. One saw them streaming in the doors, treading lightly, eyes lifted to catch a glimpse of her, smiles of anticipation lighting every face; then after the meeting moving reluctantly away, recalling the wit and charm and drollery, then the kernel of the speech, convinced of its wisdom and adopting it as their own immediate program. Or she was the center of a delegation to a national convention at Des Moines, Buffalo or Richmond, or representing the League at the International Woman's Suffrage Alliance abroad. Questions of women's nationality and citizenship concerned her.

These pictures are far afield and they are close at home. They all have a center, youth, the rights of childhood. Nor was she uncertain of the future. "In one form," she said, "sooner or later as we decree by our interest or its lack, the child will win. This is our opportunity to keep up and keep on with our eyes wider open and our minds better informed and our courage stouter."

Miss Lathrop also served as chairman of the National Child Welfare Committee and as a member of the National Board of the League of Women Voters. A member of the latter relates that during a committee discussion of the Sheppard-Towner bill advocating pre-natal care and other safeguards for child-bearing women, someone broke out with the query, "Why is it that the Congressmen are so obstinate about this bill?" A member replied, "It is of course 'the curse' laid upon Eve, with all its physiological and theological implications," whereupon Julia Lathrop said with a sigh, "'The curse' was the very worst thing that happened in that garden, and to have it still determining the course of human events is even more trying because it couldn't possibly have happened."

Of the League she wrote:

> The League of Women Voters urges women to join and work in the parties of their choice, but first to have a choice based on something more than tradition or prejudice or sentiment. Only in one way can an intelligent vote be made—the hard road of study and thought. Hence Schools of Citizenship. It cannot be done either by mere looking on—we must both study and take part. Nor can study and work be abstract. Study leads to decisions which we support by our work.
>
> The League endeavors to make plain the value of what might be called the laboratory or experimental side of political education, taking due share in such work as registration, getting out the vote, action as election judges, framing party platforms, examining the qualifications of candidates. It urges women to become candidates under whatever party banners best satisfy their minds, believing that the campaign where opinions and platforms are examined and defended has long proved itself a vast educational power.

To the end she urged better administration of existing laws.

> We are still indifferent to the quality of public service. A merit system of appointments is evaded whenever and wherever possible. Yet a merit system means only some effective method of securing competent honest public servants, such methods as any successful administration of private business must employ.
>
> Public business has vastly increased in scope since the first civil service laws were written in the United States fifty years or so ago. The present juncture with the growing tendency to enact social legislation is crucial in its need of a new public conscience as to Public Administration.

During these all too infrequent visits at Hull-House we also discussed the vexed subject of Prohibition which threatened after the war to submerge the consideration of all other public questions. Her experience was much too varied and her mind too subtle to be content with the dogmatic position taken by either side of the controversy. She instinctively disliked the entire restrictive aspect in such legislation born from abstract convictions ignoring the essential soundness of human nature itself which day by day instinctively keeps a balance between high idealism and human experience.

Yet it was this very human experience which led her to champion the retention of the amendment. She remembered a year in Rockford when the town was voting to change from dry to wet that a large group of Swedish women daily held fervent prayer meetings petitioning the good Lord to save them and their children from the horrors of drunken husbands and fathers. She could never forget her experience as a visitor in Cook County with the wretched families who had been brought to applying for county relief because the wage earner had been incapacitated by "the drink," the terrorized children who had once seen delirium tremens and did not know when the unbearable experience would recur. She had known also in every state institution for the insane in Illinois men and women brought there through alcoholism which had ruined their minds as well as their bodies and had often perverted their finest instincts. All such experiences made her cling to the experiment of prohibition in spite of its drawbacks and failures because it was obvious to anyone who knew working people that there was much less drinking among them during this period than there had been before. She hoped with most of the settlement people under whose auspices the book, "Does Prohibition Work?" was published in 1927, that the United States of America having weathered the first seven years of difficulties and at last gotten civil service regulations established for the men actually enforcing the measure, would go through the next seven years certainly more successfully. I recall discussing the book with her, which the chairman of the settlement committee, Lillian D. Wald, described as: "Not a scientific study but realistic stories conscientiously and carefully prepared by social workers in the settlements and by affiliated organizations from Maine to California. It should provide a close-up view not possible in the argumentative presentations which have been offered to the public."

Julia Lathrop was in Washington during the days when it was said that the amendment would never have been passed unless the Congressmen had been assured that its administration would at least offer a chance for good appointments in a new field for governmental agents. The members of the Anti-Saloon League also did not want the administration of the Volstead Act put under civil service regulation because they were sure their own members could enforce the law better than anyone else; they had assumed that the law enforcement would be in the hands of the people who had secured the constitutional amendment and the enabling act. Between Congressmen wishing positions for their henchmen and the Anti-Saloon League desiring to place their own members in office because no one else could be trusted, the administration of the Volstead Act got the worst kind of start with no civil service safeguards whatever.

I once heard her say at a dinner table discussion of civil service reform that it might have been better under these circumstances if the amendment had never been passed, for now we should never really know what the result of Prohibition would have been under an adequate and reasonable administration of the law. She added whimsically, that no law should be considered "passed" by Congress without an examination, either medical or lay, to ascertain whether or not the Congressmen had held their tongues in their cheeks as they voted.

I find it difficult to reproduce her position on another aspect of Prohibition. She disliked as much as I did a certain self-righteousness in the good citizen when he voted for laws which he himself had no intention of obeying, as the southern man voted for the Eighteenth Amendment because he wanted to keep drink away from the Negro, the northern manufacturer because he wished sober immigrant labor, and so on. Such voting resulted in a law regarded as an instrument for making other people good, the very antithesis of democracy. It was perhaps an outgrowth of the discussion on Prohibition that led to my conversation with her on the widespread desire for conformity which characterized this country after the war. It is hard to tell what actually produced such a situation. Doubtless fear of Russia was an element in it but certainly for a decade there was less scope for individual self-expression within the ordered framework of the state than there ever had been before on American soil. She was distressed by the situation, as every broadminded citizen was, and said in one of her addresses: "The present time is one in which it requires unusual courage to be courageous. A weary acceptance of apparent defeat is easier."

It was in connection with this situation that we once recalled the treatment of John Lothrop which was more or less typical of that ac-

corded to all dissenters whose beliefs outraged Bishop Laud and his orthodox following. At that period all men felt as strongly and were as
easily driven to persecution in regard to religious beliefs as at the moment we appeared to be in regard to differing social theories. It did not
seem more reprehensible to the orthodox that they should track down
the heretics who were worshiping according to the dictates of their own
consciences than it seemed improper to present day holders of established social views that they should raid the headquarters of the "reds"
and arrest as large a number of them as possible. She made the observation that it was always easy to be liberal for any cause except the contemporary one but that that was after all the real test of liberality. She
added: "What a different world we might have had if Archbishop Laud
who imprisoned the Puritans, including my own ancestor, and Oliver
Cromwell who beheaded Archbishop Laud, had been able to compre-
hend Bacon's conception of a spiritual union founded on variety and
liberty."

The last months of her life were filled with concern over the impending execution of a young criminal from Rockford who was still a minor
in years and certainly in development. She possessed that horror over
the deliberate taking of life on the part of the state which has overshadowed some of the greatest minds in each generation during the
last two centuries. For Julia Lathrop, so long identified with governmental service in the county, the state and the nation, official violence
such as an execution held almost an element of complicity on her part
which must have been well-nigh unendurable.

In August 1931 Russell McWilliams, a seventeen-year-old Rockford
boy, held up the passengers on a streetcar, shooting and killing the mo-
torman. He was arrested the next day and charged with murder. At the
first trial in the circuit court Russell pleaded guilty and was sentenced
to be electrocuted in December 1931. A few days after the sentence Julia
Lathrop wrote a public letter which contains the following: "Such a
death sentence pronounced against a boy of that age is against public
policy. Condemning to death so young and undeveloped a person is a
profound miscarriage of justice." She immediately organized an appeal against the execution of minors which became nation-wide. Many

letters and petitions were sent to the Governor of Illinois and publicity was obtained through several powerful newspapers whose policy was against capital punishment. Miss Lathrop with an attorney from Rockford, two distinguished attorneys from Chicago, and Jessie F. Binford, the Superintendent of the Juvenile Protective Association, undertook the responsibility for the boy's legal defense and also for financing the case. This was the beginning of one of the most widely publicized trials of a juvenile in the United States, lasting from October 1931 to April 1933, with three trials in the Rockford Circuit Court each of which resulted in a death sentence, two appeals in the Illinois Supreme Court each of which resulted in remanding the case for retrial. The Illinois Supreme Court remanded the case to the Rockford court on the ground that "further testimony should be heard in mitigation as well as aggravation," and reminded the lower court that the youth of the defendant entitled him to special consideration in fixing the penalty. Appeals to two Illinois governors—as an election had taken place during the year and a half—followed two hearings before the State Board of Pardons where the case was ably presented.

Among the last letters Julia Lathrop wrote was one to Jessie Binford in regard to this case, dated April 4, 1932, just before she went to the hospital, as follows: "Unless signs fail, I am likely to go to the hospital next week. . . . Of course it is not really serious, but it would be impracticable even I can see, to be in a hospital and in the presence of the Governor simultaneously. I am sorry it all happens that way." As a postscript to the same letter she added: "I can be counted upon to bear the expenses of the trip from Boston and return of one, if that last appeal becomes necessary as I think likely. If we could have both Van Waters and Healy it would be the best help in the country, probably in the world."

On April 9th she writes again from Rockford to Jessie Binford: "I don't know what to advise until after the Supreme Court decision. . . . Of course I feel that it is not a legal question any more." On the morning of April 15th, the very day of Julia Lathrop's death, Jessie Binford wrote to the boy in Joliet: "Miss Julia Lathrop of Rockford who, although you do not know it, has probably done more than anyone else to help you, is very ill. She wrote me just before she had an operation on Tuesday that she would go with me down to see you as soon as she got better." So the last journey that Julia Lathrop planned was to the state penitentiary, one of the institutions she knew very well as a member of the early State Board and which had been designated as the place for the boy's execution.

The last time I saw Julia Lathrop she had come to Hull-House to see Jessie Binford, as the Juvenile Protective Association, of which she was the superintendent, has its offices in one of the Hull-House buildings. Julia Lathrop came out from the office quite disturbed and said to me, "Of course, J.A., you and I have long stood against capital punishment, with a great many other people, but apparently no one has made any impression upon the people of Illinois. The whole legal system feels positively virtuous about its so-called severity and regards the abolition of the death penalty as sheer sentimentality. They do not stop to inquire if capital punishment has ever proved a deterrent to crime." She added something to the effect that of course no human being can ever hope to be absolutely just, but that there are degrees of fallibility, and why should men keep alive such a hideous custom founded upon the superstitions and fears of an earlier stage of human development and refuse to accept the findings of scientific inquiries made in various parts of the world. She concluded with the remark that governmental agencies have been proverbially belated in recognizing the findings of science but that such slow progress against traditionalism is never so painfully portrayed as in the retention of capital punishment.

As Julia Lathrop had planned, Dr. Miriam Van Waters came from Massachusetts to examine the boy and afterwards carried on a correspondence with him from which the following excerpts are taken. He wrote often about his dog which seemed to be much on his mind during his imprisonment in the state penitentiary. In one letter he wrote: "I have not heard anything about my dog, but Mom says the family is well, so that means the dog is also well. He plays with the little kids, also watches them, very suspicious of the strangers." Again he writes: "It is tough about my dog. It is bad enough about me but my dog never harmed anyone. He was very good." In a later letter: "I hear from home quite often. Things are dead back there. Mike is still getting a little work. Dad can't find nothing to do. I don't know if I am going to be able to keep my religion or not. I've did the best I could, and some time ago I never thought I would ever slide back; but I never knew then what I know now."

On May 23rd when the date set for his execution was drawing near the boy wrote: "God will take care of me. The old devil Satan cannot take me unless God says it is O.K." Then he wrote Dr. Van Waters again: "The truth is that I don't expect any 30–day stay. Mother and I were arranging things for my funeral. It was a terrible thing to talk about, but just in case I did die I wanted to know."

On April 13, 1933, the newly elected Governor of Illinois, acting on the recommendation of his new Pardon Board, commuted the sentence of Russell McWilliams from death to imprisonment for 99 years. This commutation was issued a year after Julia Lathrop's death in the Rockford hospital on April 15, 1932.

14

Tributes to Julia Clifford Lathrop, April 15, 1932

❧ From the many tributes paid to her in that sad April of 1932 from the President of the United States and hundreds of public men and individuals, I shall select a few dealing with her life before she went to Washington. The first is from a Rockford paper, homely and personal:

The Rockford *Register-Republic,* speaking for local interest in the career which had "formed one of the brightest stories in the achievements of American women," declares that "her life has been a source of pride to this community in which she was born," and recalls that "she could have lived a life of ease, indifferent to the problems of society, indulging herself in a placid and aimless existence, but her cultured mind and high spirit dictated a vastly different career." The Rockford paper adds:

> It was immensely gratifying to Miss Lathrop's fellow townsmen that her transcendent ability had widespread recognition. Curiously enough, although she was a member of an old Republican family, it was a Democratic Governor, John P. Altgeld, who was the first to draw her into the service of the state. A Democratic President, Woodrow Wilson, refused to remove her from the post of Chief of the Federal Children's Bureau to which she had been appointed by President Taft. Miss Lathrop was vouchsafed a long life, but she lived 'in deeds, not years.' Of rare intellectual gifts, she bore herself with the unpretentiousness that is so real in the truly accomplished. She had a happy wit and gaiety of spirit and her friends loved her greatly for her personal charm.
>
> She was born with that gift of human sympathy which, more

than any other single quality, gives approach to hearts and supports frail lives.

By study and constant effort she made herself well informed in the ways of help, especially for more considerate care of the insane, for the health and happiness of children, for the guidance and reform of youthful delinquents. . . .

At Hull-House and elsewhere, unremittingly, unobtrusively and effectively, she kept on giving out strength to the weak, bringing light into darkened lives, leading those who had erred back to safer and happier ways. Miss Lathrop made a career out of kindness.

Dr. Graham Taylor, her friend and colleague for many years, wrote for the *Chicago Daily News:*

Julia Lathrop's only claim for what she did was that it was due from her as a citizen. Before women's citizenship was legally recognized by conceding their right to the suffrage she was as conscious of the community's claim upon her as she was of her own personality. This community consciousness was hers by birthright in a family which shared and served the life of the home and state, whose father represented them in the congress of the nation.

She saw citizenship as she saw life, whole. While at every stage of its development she sought local basis for her action, yet no part she took obscured her view on the whole horizon of which it was a part. In this firm, far-reaching grasp of an entire situation her statesmanship was widely recognized.

From Rockford and Vassar Colleges she came to Chicago to share with her college mate, Jane Addams, the point of view and of contact afforded by the experience of living and working with cosmopolitan neighbors of Hull-House during the second year of its adventurous career. There nothing was so lowly as to be apart from the vision taken of civic obligation and opportunity. While social justice and opportunity for immigrant neighbors made the first appeal to the settlement residents, Miss Lathrop accepted the county agent's appointment to be a volunteer visitor to the homes of all the applicants for relief within ten blocks of Hull-House. Her sense of the state's responsibility for the care of its wards was thus deepened and broadened. They became her wards, as a citizen responsible for the public care of the destitute child, the aged person and the insane.

One, from the *New York Herald Tribune,* emphasizes the pioneer aspect of her activities:

Julia Lathrop belonged to the vanishing race of pioneer women to whom the world of 1932 is indebted for many reform measures which it has come almost to take for granted, yet which were won only through a degree of human courage and devotion which can never be taken for granted. Miss Lathrop was, of course, not of the first generation of pioneers who exposed themselves to public ridicule by attempting to speak in behalf of women's right to education or political independence. She was the beneficiary of their labors, inasmuch as she was graduated from Vassar College in 1880, when the woman movement was already in its second phase.

For more than fifty years, however, she carried on the work which the early pioneers had started, until her name throughout the land became a symbol of altruism coupled with a passion for scientific and orderly thinking. She was a crusader who worked through legislative processes. In the Illinois State Board of Charities, to which she was appointed as long ago as 1893, she led campaigns for the abolition through law of child labor, for the establishment of juvenile courts, factory inspection, tenement house reforms and the improved management of state and county charitable institutions. When she was appointed by President Taft in 1912 as the head of the Children's Bureau she was the first woman to hold an important federal post. In 1925, although ill health had caused her to resign her heavy duties in Washington, she became an assessor-member of the advisory committee on child welfare of the League of Nations, a post she held until last December.

Thus she worked for fifty years with a spiritual zeal that never flagged, and which one is sometimes tempted to say has gone out of fashion in these softer times. However, Julia Lathrop and Jane Addams and Lillian D. Wald developed in the gay nineties just as Anna Howard Shaw and Susan B. Anthony were the children of the hoop-skirt and smelling salts era; so, probably, a new race of pioneers is growing up amid the cigarette smoke and petting parties.

Index

of, 77–80; merit system vs., xiii, xviii–
xix; prohibition's passage and, 148–49;
at state and county institutions, 51–52,
63–64, 66–67
Penn, William, 120
Peoria hospital for the insane, 68
Peterson, Frederick, 114
Philanthropy and Social Progress (book),
41
Philippine Islands: child welfare in, 138–39
phospohorous: dangers of, 135–36
Plato Club, xii, 37
Plymouth School (Mass.), 39–41
Podstata, Vaclav H., 70–73
political parties. *See* patronage appointments
politics: of Children's Bureau, xxii; corruption in, 71–72; differences vs. conformity in, 149–50; frustrations with,
63–64, 66–68, 88; immigration and,
127–28; of prohibition, 148–49; skills
in, xvi–xvii; violence associated with,
129; women's responsibility in, 144–48
poorhouse ("infirmary"): daily life in,
xiii; as last resort, 49; older people in,
50–51; in southern county, 65; staff of,
51–52. *See also* poverty and poor people
Potter, Adeline. *See* Lathrop, Adeline
Potter (mother)
Potter, Adeline Lathrop (great-aunt), 7, 8
Potter, Andrew (uncle), 26
Potter, Edward Eells (uncle), 10, 12–13
Potter, Eleazer Hubbell (grandfather):
arrival of, 10–11; description of, 11–13;
financial difficulties of, 17
Potter, Henry (great-uncle), 11–12
Potter, Joel, 7, 16
Potter, Mark (great-uncle), 11–12
Potter, Mary Morrell (stepmother), 11
Potter, (Sarah) Adeline Eells (grand-
mother), 10, 11
poverty and poor people: in Asia, 136, 140;
attitudes toward, xx–xxii; compassion
for, 48–50; neighborhood of, described,
49–50, 53–54; persistence of, xxix
Preston & Potter (store), 11
professionalism: focus on, xvi; public service and, 86–87. *See also* social sci-
ences

Prohibition, xvii, 147–49
prostitute: child's custody and, 121–22
Psychopathic Institution for Children:
founding of, xv, 99–100, 114; history
of, 94
public service: European examples of,
76–77; inclusiveness as ideal in, 66; interest in developing, 86–87; Lathrop's
and school of philanthropy's role in,
111–13; quality of, 52–53, 147. *See also*
county and state institutions
Pullman Company, 103, 126

Quezon, Manuel, 45

Ramabai, Pundita, 133
Rapp, John N., 80–81
Red Scare, xxvi–xxvii
Relief and Aid Society, 54–55
religious differences: immigration due
to, 5–6, 37; in Lathrop family, 132, 138;
political differences compared with,
149–50; politics and, 19–21
Republican Party, xviii, xxiv, 15, 20
research: by Children's Bureau, xx; focus
on, xvi; on juveniles, 99; as means not
end, xvii; university department for,
xv, 108–9, 112–13
Rew, Robert, 28
Rich, Mrs. Kenneth, 45, 125, 144–46
Rivington Street settlement (N.Y.C.), 39
Rockford (Ill.): alcohol laws in, 148; ante-
bellum growth of, 12; area of, 10–11;
capital punishment case in, 150–53;
childhood years in, 25–28; immigrants
in, 21–22; incorporation of, 10; indus-
trialization of, 23–24, 34; opportunities
in, 7, 10; public education in, 25–26, 28;
speech on, 56–58; street lighting controversy in, 18; watch factories in, 57
Rockford College (earlier, Rockford Female Seminary): Addams's speech at,
35; Hull-House summer school at, 23,
56; staff of, 32, 34; students of, 13–14,
125–28; theatrical efforts at, 27–28;
trustees of, 18
Rockford *Register-Republic*, 154–55
Rock River, 56–57
Roosevelt, Franklin D., xxiv, xxvii, xxviii

Japan, 139; Philippines, 138–39; Scotland, xiv, 73, 74–77
Trumbull, Lyman, 21
tuberculosis, 114
Typographical Union, 103

United Charities, 54
U.S. Bureau of Labor, 48
U.S. Congress: child labor amendment and, xxiv; Children's Bureau and, xviii, xix, xxii; Lathrop's father in, 22; prohibition and, 148–49
U.S. Constitution, xxiv, 85
U.S. Department of Labor, 127–28
U.S. Indian Service, 87
U.S. Supreme Court, xxiii, 85
universities: closing gap between daily life and, 34
University of Chicago: graduate school of social work at, xvi, 111; graduate students at, 128; sociology at, 40
University of Chicago Press, 113
Upton, Harriet Taylor, xxiv

Van Waters, Miriam, 151, 152, 153
Vassar College: as influence, xii; Lathrop at, 28–29, 32–34; memorial to Lathrop at, 32; School of Euthenics at, 29–31
Veyra, Madame Jaime C. de, 138–39
violence: stereotypes of, 128–29
Volstead Act (Prohibition), xvii, 147–49
voluntary associations (all-female): Children's Bureau linked to, xix–xx; emergence of, ix; impetus for, xiv–xv; relationships with, 118–30. See also specific organizations

Wald, Lillian D.: child labor and, xxiv; Children's Bureau and, xviii; circle of, x, 156; mental hygiene and, 114; mentioned, 92; on prohibition, 148; on statistics on children, 119
Ward, Grace, 131–32
war orphans, 60. See also Civil War; Great War
Watertown hospital for the insane, 68
Weber, Col. George, 56–57

Weiss, Nancy P., xxxi–xxxii n. 29
Wellesley College, 111
white slave trade, 83, 124
Wickersham, George W., 129
Wiebe, Robert, xxx n. 14
Wilson, Woodrow: child labor bill and, xxiii; election of, xviii–xix; labor conference under, 134–35; Lathrop's relationship with, xxii, 154
woman suffrage: goals of, xxv, xxvi; in India, 137; responsibility associated with, 144–46; support for, 19, 103, 143–44. See also National League of Women Voters
women: death of, 49; differences among, xx–xxi, xxiv; immigration of unaccompanied, 124–25; in India, 136–37; opportunities for, xix, 68–69; organizations of, 118–30; political participation and voting of, 144–48; rights of, 19, 20, 31. See also woman suffrage; women workers
Women Patriots, xxvi–xxvii
Women's Christian Temperance Union, xxvi, xxvii
Women's Joint Congressional Committee, xxiv, xxvi
Women's Trade Union League, 43
Women's Union Missionary Society, 19, 131
women workers: case of insane, 116; in mills, 102–3; protective legislation for, 84–85, 88
Woods, Robert A., 39
working class: housing for, 102; interest in, x; mental hygiene of, 115–17. See also labor force; tenements; women workers
World's Fairs. See Columbian Exposition (1893); Paris Exposition
World War I. See Great War

Yale University, 32
Yates, Richard, xvii, 77–80
Year of the Child, xxiii, xxvii
Young, Ella Flagg, 118
youth. See children and youth

Zeisler, Fannie Bloomfield, 118

JANE ADDAMS (1860–1935) was a social activist, a leading Progressive reformer, public speaker, author of many books of social criticism, and an original theorist who contributed to the development of American sociology and pragmatist philosophy. Her feminism, pacifism, and pragmatist experimentalism found concrete expression in the institutions she founded or to which she gave early support, including the Hull-House settlement in Chicago, the National Association for the Advancement of Colored People, the National American Woman Suffrage Association, the American Civil Liberties Union, and the Woman's International League for Peace and Freedom. She was awarded the Nobel Peace Prize in 1931.

ANNE FIROR SCOTT, professor emerita of history at Duke University and one of the pioneers of women's history, is the author of numerous books, among them *Unheard Voices, Natural Allies: Women's Associations in American History,* and *Making the Invisible Woman Visible.*

The University of Illinois Press
is a founding member of the
Association of American University Presses.

———————————————————————

Composed in 10.5/13 Adobe Minion
with Nueva display
by Type One, LLC
for the University of Illinois Press
Manufactured by Sheridan Books, Inc.

University of Illinois Press
1325 South Oak Street
Champaign, IL 61820-6903
www.press.uillinois.edu